Thai
cooking

The Confident Cooking Promise of Success

Welcome to the world of Confident Cooking,
where recipes are double-tested by our team
of home economists to achieve a high standard
of success—and delicious results every time.

bay books

C O N T

Chicken Curry Puffs, page 26

Fish Fillets in Coconut Milk, page 43

Thai Fried Noodles, page 65

Spicy Roasted Eggplant with Tofu, page 81

All recipes in this book have been double-tested.

Green Pawpaw and Peanut Salad, page 80

Watercress and Duck Salad with Lychees, page 91

The Publisher thanks the following for their assistance in the photography for this book:

Balgowlah Heights Fruit & Flowers
Cambur Industries
Country Road
Dinosaur Designs
Dulux Paints
Gourmet Tarts
Grace Bros/Myers
Home & Garden
Noritake
Pontip Asian Foods
Ridgeway Sasella & Partners
Royal Doulton
Wedgwood

When we test our recipes, we rate them for ease of preparation. The following cookery ratings are on the recipes in this book, making them easy to use and understand.

A single Cooking with Confidence symbol indicates a recipe that is simple and generally quick to make – perfect for beginners.

Two symbols indicate the need for just a little more care and a little more time.

Three symbols indicate special dishes that need more investment in time, care and patience—but the results are worth it.

NOTES
International conversions and a glossary explaining unfamiliar terms can be found on page 112. Cooking times may vary slightly depending on the individual oven. We suggest you check the manufacturer's instructions to ensure proper temperature control.

Spicy Coconut Custard, page 107

Bananas in Lime Juice with Coconut Pancakes, page 108

A Thai Table

Thai cuisine has become familiar to the Western world through restaurants, and most people can order comfortably from a Thai menu, or quote favourite dishes. Now, with the growing availability of Thai ingredients, these dishes can be easily re-created at home. Thai food strikes a balance between sweet, sour, hot, bitter and salty. Taste each dish before serving and adjust seasonings to suit. The word *Thai* means 'free', and Thai cooks always add their own special touches to every dish.

● PLANNING THE MENU

In Thailand the various dishes which make up a meal are served all at once. These components may include one or more of each of the following: a soup, a curry dish, a stir-fry, a salad, accompanying sauces or dips, and of course, plenty of rice. When planning the menu, a good rule of thumb is to allow one 'main' dish per person, remembering to provide a variety of flavours and textures between each. All the dishes are placed together on the table for the diners to help themselves. The meal normally finishes with a selection of fresh tropical fruit or a sticky rice dessert.

● INGREDIENTS

If you love cooking and enjoy experimenting with new flavours, you will find Thai food very satisfying. Always use the freshest ingredients possible. Makrut (kaffir) lime leaves, galangal, lemon grass, coriander (cilantro) roots and other unusual fresh ingredients, used often in Thai cookery, are available from Asian speciality shops and some greengrocers. If you can't see an

ingredient that you need, ask your greengrocer to obtain it for you. A lot of the other ingredients, particularly the sauces and noodles, are now available in supermarkets. The pictures in the glossary will help with identification. Don't be intimidated by having to find unusual ingredients, but seek them out and explore new areas for shopping. The 'heat' of spicy dishes may be adjusted according to personal taste but, remember, chillies are included in dishes for flavour, not just for their heat, and so too much or too little may alter a dish considerably.

● RICE

Rice is very important in Thai cooking and is included at all meals, except quick snacks. The best variety to use for a Thai meal is jasmine rice, which has a delicate fragrance. Salt is not added to the rice as the other dishes in the meal will be seasoned sufficiently. Rice is the staple, not an accompaniment, and all the other dishes served at the meal, including the meat dishes, are seen as condiments to flavour the rice. It's important that the rice stays hot throughout the meal so it can be kept covered, if you like.

● EQUIPMENT

A few simple pieces of equipment help to make Thai cookery easier. A couple of woks—large and small, with lids if possible—are desirable, although large heavy-based frying pans can be used. You will need a little extra oil when using a frying pan because of the larger surface area. Woks vary from relatively expensive stainless steel to more simple ones made with cheaper metal. Flat-bottomed woks are best for electric stoves as they sit more securely. Traditional rolled-steel woks need to be oiled to prevent them from rusting between uses, whereas non-stick woks are easily maintained.

A wooden spoon is adequate for stir-frying, or you can buy an implement called a wok charn which has a wide, flat end. Avoid using a plastic spatula, and if your wok has a non-stick surface, use wooden rather than metal implements. Tongs or a slotted spoon are necessary for removing fried foods from hot oil, though a traditional wire mesh strainer with a wooden handle is best as the wooden handle does not conduct heat, and the open mesh allows the oil to drain away easily. Bamboo steamers, available from Asian speciality stores, are inexpensive and make steaming very simple. A large mortar and pestle, or a small-bowled food processor, is essential for curry pastes and for pounding ingredients such as garlic, ginger, galangal and lemon grass. A clean coffee grinder is handy for grinding small amounts of dry spices. And, of course, a couple of sturdy chopping boards and sharp knives are a must.

Clockwise from top: Fruit Platter (page 105); Hot and Sour Prawn Soup (page 29); Vegetarian Rice Noodles (page 71); Crisp Whole Fish with Sour Pepper and Coriander Sauce (page 58); Steamed Rice (page 68); Hot Pork Curry with Pumpkin (page 44)

Thai Glossary

Many of the ingredients necessary for Thai cookery are
not easily attainable but the extra effort you make to find them
will be rewarded with wonderful exotic flavours.

Thai cuisine is a surprising blend of sweet, sour and hot flavours. Small amounts of individual components blend to create the subtle yet distinctive flavours. Speciality Asian food stores as well as some greengrocers and supermarkets stock some of the more obscure ingredients used in Thai cookery. In capital cities that have a Chinatown area, there are wonderful stores worth exploring, not only for the ingredients, but also for reasonably priced, commonly used utensils, such as woks and steaming baskets. Of course, you can use alternative equipment quite successfully.

BARBECUED PORK

These are spit-roasted cuts of pork, available from Chinese barbecue shops. Also known as **char siu**. Honey smoked ham can be substituted.

BASIL

There are three varieties of basil that are used in Thai cuisine. **Bai Horapha** tastes rather like anise, looks like sweet basil, and is used in red and green curries. **Bai Manglaek** has a lemony flavour, tiny leaves and is usually sprinkled over salads or used in soups. **Bai Grapao** has a clove-like taste and purple-reddish tinged leaves. It doesn't store well, so buy just before you intend to use it. European basil can be used as a substitute for all varieties if you can't find the Thai varieties. Basil has a strong flavour, so don't use more than the recipe states. Some nurseries sell Thai basil, so try growing your own.

BEAN CURD (Tofu)

Tofu is made from soya beans and is an excellent source of protein. A creamy-white, firm tofu is sold in blocks, wrapped in plastic, and is used in soups, stir-fries and salads. Fried tofu is golden brown on the outside, a little rubbery in texture, and is added to salads and used as a garnish for soups. Fresh tofu doesn't have much taste when uncooked but absorbs other flavours. It should be refrigerated in water that is changed daily and used within a few days of purchase.

BEAN SPROUTS

Used mainly in salads and as a stir-fry vegetable, sprouts are crunchy, white and short. Discard any that are limp or brown. They are highly perishable so use within three days of purchase. Traditionally, the scraggly ends are removed.

BLACK FUNGUS

This is a Chinese ingredient used in some Thai dishes. It has no flavour but is used for its texture. It is a member of the mushroom family, available in dried form, and looks like dried, black, wrinkled paper. When soaked in water for about 10 minutes, it swells and resembles wavy seaweed or jelly. Stored in its dried form, it will keep indefinitely.

CARDAMOM

An aromatic spice of Indian origin, available as whole seeds, whole pods, or ground. It has a strong, fresh flavour and is an important ingredient of Musaman curry, a Thai dish with a Persian influence.

CHILLIES

Chillies are a common ingredient in Thai cuisine, although not all dishes are hot. Chillies come in a great variety of sizes, shapes and colours, and are available fresh and dried, as flakes and powder. The most commonly used fresh chillies are bird's-eye chillies—small, thin, green, or sometimes red, chillies. Generally, the larger the chilli the milder the flavour—the very tiny red chillies can be very hot. To avoid skin irritation, take great care when seeding or chopping chillies—wear rubber gloves. After handling chillies don't touch your face, eyes or any tender part of the body and always wash your hands thoroughly. If you like a hot curry, leave the seeds in, but if you prefer a milder flavour, the seeds can be removed to lessen the heat. Whole chillies freeze well in plastic bags and can be chopped frozen. Some chillies are available dried and are usually soaked in water, to soften, before use.

CHILLI JAM OR PASTE

Chilli jam is a sweet and sourish tangy jam that is sold in jars at Asian food stores. It is used in sauces, stir-fries and some soups. After opening, store it in the refrigerator.

CHINESE DRIED MUSHROOMS

These impart a very distinct flavour to the dish and are used in Thai dishes that have a Chinese influence. They need to be soaked before use and are available from Asian food stores. Store in a sealed container in a cool place.

CHINESE CABBAGE

Also known as wom bok. This has pale green leaves and a slight mustard flavour. If unavailable, use another curly-leaf cabbage.

COCONUT MILK, COCONUT CREAM

Coconut milk is extracted from the flesh of fresh coconuts—it is not the clear, watery liquid found in the centre of fresh coconuts. **Coconut cream** is quite thick, almost of a spreadable consistency. It is the product of the first extraction from the flesh. It is very rich and is usually added at the end of cooking time to enrich the curry or sauce or dessert. **Coconut milk** is a thinner consistency than the cream as it is extracted from the flesh after the cream has already been produced. It is used in Thai curries and desserts. Good quality, canned coconut milk and cream are available from Asian food stores and supermarkets. Some brands call the thinner consistency coconut cream, so try different ones until you find the right consistency. Sometimes coconut milk separates and the fat solidifies on the top—if this happens, just stir it well. Once the can is opened the milk or cream doesn't keep, so freeze any leftovers in small amounts for future use.

Dried coconut milk is available in packets and can be made the desired consistency and richness by following the directions on the packet; it also has a good storage life. If you can't buy any coconut cream or milk, you can make it using desiccated coconut. Pour 3 cups of hot water over 550 g (1 lb 4 oz) desiccated coconut; allow to stand for 15 minutes and strain through a fine sieve or muslin, squeezing as much liquid as possible out of the coconut. The product from this first extraction is used wherever coconut cream is called for. Repeat the process, using the same coconut to make the thinner coconut milk.

CORIANDER

Also known as **cilantro**, coriander is the most common herb used in Thai cooking. The whole plant is used— the root, stem and leaves. The seeds are roasted and then ground in a spice mill and used in curry pastes. Fresh coriander is available from Asian food stores, greengrocers, or in pots from plant nurseries. The leaves are used for their fresh, peppery flavour, and as a garnish. For storage, wash and dry the fresh herbs before placing them in plastic bags in the refrigerator—they will keep for 5–6 days. Dried coriander is not a suitable substitute.

CRISP FRIED ONION AND GARLIC

These are finely sliced garlic cloves or onions that have been deep-fried until crisp. They are added to soups, noodle dishes or salads just before serving. They are available in jars from Asian food stores or you can prepare them by finely slicing peeled onion and garlic and cooking over low heat in oil, stirring regularly until crisp and golden-brown. Drain well and allow to cool before seasoning with salt. This should be done just before serving.

CUMIN

This is an aromatic spice with a distinctive flavour and aroma, used in curry pastes. You can buy whole seeds or ground powder. The cumin seed is roasted and then ground in a spice mill before using in curry pastes.

DRIED CHINESE DATES

Sweet and salty dates used in Chinese-style soups and casseroles, available from Asian food stores. Store in a jar in a cool place.

DRIED SHIMP

Tiny salted shrimp that have been dried in the sun. They are used for flavour, especially in sauces.

EGGPLANTS

Also known as **aubergines**, eggplants of many different sizes, shapes and colours are used in Thai cooking. Tiny pea-sized eggplants available in some Asian food stores are often used—they can be bitter in flavour. Small, long lady-finger eggplants are also used. European eggplants may substituted.

FISH SAUCE (Nam Pla)

This brown, salty sauce with a characteristic 'fishy' smell is an important ingredient in Thai cookery. It is made from prawns (shrimp) or small fish which have been fermented in the sun for a long time. It is readily available and there really is no substitute. Store in the refrigerator after opening.

FRENCH SHALLOTS
(Eschallots)

These come in small clusters, like garlic, and are brown in colour. Shallots are an important ingredient in Thai cooking and it is even better, of course, if you can find **Asian shallots** which are a similar shape and size but are purple or red in colour. Large red or brown onions can be used as a substitute.

GALANGAL
(Laos)

Related to ginger and looks quite similar, but is pinkish and has a distinct peppery flavour. Used in curry pastes, stir-fries and soups. Available fresh and dried from Asian food stores and fresh from some greengrocers. Use fresh galangal if possible and be careful when handling that you don't get the juice on your clothes or hands as it stains. Dried galangal must be soaked in hot water before use.

GARLIC

An indispensable ingredient in Thai cookery, it is available in different varieties, some with very white papery skin, some with pink and white skin and some creamy in colour. Choose cloves about 1 cm (1/2 inch) wide, otherwise adjust the quantity as some cloves are up to 2.5 cm (1 inch) wide.

GARLIC CHIVES

Garlic-scented, flat-sided thick chives that have an edible flower. They need very little cooking and are usually added to soups, noodle dishes, stir-fries or salads just before serving. If unavailable, use normal chives.

GINGER

A delicious, aromatic ingredient, important in Thai cooking. Fresh ginger is readily available—buy firm, unwrinkled rhizomes and store them in a plastic bag so they don't dry out.

GOLDEN MOUNTAIN SAUCE

This is a thin, salty, spicy sauce that is made from soya beans. It is available from some Asian speciality shops. However, as this sauce may be difficult to obtain the recipes in this book use soy sauce as a substitute.

GREEN MANGO AND GREEN PAWPAW

These are commonly used in Thai salads and some soups, or as a snack with sugar and chilli—they are not a different variety but are underripe. Green mango is used for the tartness and texture which is very different to the ripe fruit—ripe mangoes are not a suitable substitute so, if necessary, use very tart green apples.

GREEN OR PINK PEPPERCORNS

Peppercorns that are bottled or canned in a brine. The peppercorns should be drained and rinsed before use. Thai and European varieties are readily available.

MAKRUT (KAFFIR) LIMES AND LEAVES

A knobbly, dark-skinned lime with a very strong lime fragrance and flavour. The leaves are finely shredded for use in curry pastes and salads, or added whole to curries. The zest is pungent and is grated over salads, soups and curries. Fresh leaves, sold in Asian food stores and speciality greengrocers, freeze well in airtight bags. Dried leaves are available from Asian food stores, but can only be added to foods which are simmered to allow the flavour to be released. If makrut (kaffir) limes are not available, standard limes may be used for zest and juice, although the flavour is not quite the same. The leaves are not suitable as a substitute for makrut (kaffir) lime leaves.

LEMON GRASS

An aromatic herb that is used in curry pastes, stir-fries and soups. Trim the base, remove the tough, outer layers, and finely slice, chop or pound the white interior. For pastes and salads, use the tender, white portion just above the root. The whole stem, trimmed and washed thoroughly, can be added to simmering soups and curries and removed before serving. Dried lemon grass needs to soak in water for half an hour before use, but the flavour of fresh is superior.

LYCHEES

Small oval fruit about the size of an unshelled walnut, with sweet, pale pink flesh similar in flavour to a grape. They have thin, knobbly, reddish skin and a brown seed. Lychees are in season during summer and are also available canned.

NOODLES

Noodles used in Asian cooking may seem confusing at first because there are so many different shapes, thickness and lengths. They are also made from different ingredients and come dried or fresh.

Fresh egg noodles, used frequently in Thai cooking, come in various thicknesses. They require a very brief cooking time. All fresh noodles can be found in the refrigerated section of most Asian food stores and some supermarkets.

Rice vermicelli are white and folded into a block. Their thickness and widths vary. They are used in stir-fries and soups, and need to be soaked in hot water or boiled until soft and then drained well before use. If they are to be used as a garnish or for the noodle dish, Mee Grob, the dried vermicelli is deep-fried until it puffs up. Rice vermicelli separate and puff up when deep-fried and a little goes a long way so always deep-fry in small quantities.

Bean vermicelli (cellophane noodles) are fine, string-like, dried transparent noodles made from mung beans. They have a firmer texture than the rice noodles once softened. In most recipes they are soaked in warm water, to soften, but sometimes they are plunged into boiling water and cooked until tender. They are used in salads, spring rolls and soups. A little goes a long way and will keep indefinitely, stored in an airtight container.

Rice stick noodles are flat. They are sold in bundles and used in noodle stir-fries and soups.

OYSTER SAUCE

A Cantonese staple found only in Thai dishes that have a Chinese influence, it is made from dried oysters. This rich, salty sauce is used for both flavour and colour, mostly in omelettes, stir-fries, soups or noodle dishes. It is readily available and should be kept refrigerated, after opening, to prevent mould forming.

PALM SUGAR

Obtained from either the palmyra palm or sugar palm, it is available in block form or in jars. The colour ranges from pale golden to very dark brown. Palm sugar is thick and crumbly and can be gently melted before adding to sauces or dressings. Soft brown sugar, demerara, or coconut sugar can be substituted, if necessary. Palm sugar is available from Asian food speciality stores.

RICE FLOUR

Rice flour is used to thicken sauces and curries or bind meat mixtures. It is also used in desserts. Cornflour can be substituted, but doesn't impart the same texture.

SESAME OIL

A very aromatic oil, made from roasted sesame seeds, used in Thai recipes that have a Chinese influence. Use it sparingly as a little goes a long way and it has quite a strong, rich flavour. Don't fry with it or use it as the only oil in a salad dressing.

SHRIMP PASTE (Blachan)

An important ingredient in Thai cooking, shrimp paste is made from dried, salted prawns (shrimps) and has a very pungent smell. Wrap in plastic wrap and store in a sealed container in the refrigerator or freezer (the refrigerator reduces the aroma, but the actual paste does not need refrigeration).

SNAKE BEANS

These are long, deep green, stringless beans, up to 30 cm (12 inches) in length. Cut in short lengths, they are used in stir-fries, curries and sometimes soups. They have less flavour than other types of green beans but are easier to prepare.

SPRING ROLL WRAPPERS

These are paper-thin wrappers, available fresh or frozen, used to make many wrapped snacks as well as spring rolls. Defrost frozen wrappers before use and keep them covered with a damp tea towel to prevent drying out.

TAMARIND

A tart-flavoured pulp that comes from the tamarind tree. It is an important ingredient in Thai cooking, and is available as a bottled purée, crystals or a pulpy solid that has to be soaked, kneaded and seeded.

TURMERIC

A bitter spice used for its intense, bright yellow-orange colour. If you use the fresh root, peel away the skin and finely grate the flesh. It is readily available in powdered form.

SUPER STARTERS

FRESH SPRING ROLLS

Preparation time: 30 minutes
Total cooking time: Nil
Makes 8

50 g (¹/₂ cup) dried rice
    vermicelli
8 dried rice paper wrappers
16 cooked prawns (shrimp),
    peeled
16 Thai basil leaves
30 g (1 cup) coriander (cilantro)
    leaves
1 medium carrot, cut into
    short thin strips
1 tablespoon grated lime zest
2 tablespoons chilli sauce
    (see pages 100–101) or
    commercial sauce

Dipping Sauce
80 ml (¹/₃ cup) cold water
1 teaspoon sugar
2 tablespoons fish sauce
1 tablespoon white vinegar
1 small red chilli, finely chopped
1 tablespoon chopped coriander
    (cilantro) leaves and stems

1 Soak the rice vermicelli in the hot water for 10 minutes and then drain. Dip a rice paper wrapper into luke-warm water, allow to soften and place on a work surface. Place 2 prawns side-by-side in the centre of the wrapper and top with 2 basil leaves, 1 tablespoon of coriander, a few carrot strips, a little lime zest and a small amount of rice noodles. Spoon a little chilli sauce over the top.

2 Press the filling down to flatten it a little; bring in two sides and roll up the parcel. Lay seam-side down on a serving plate and sprinkle with a little water; cover with plastic wrap. Repeat with remaining ingredients.

3 To make Dipping Sauce: Place the cold water in a small bowl; add the sugar and stir until it dissolves. Stir in the fish sauce, vinegar, chilli and coriander leaves and stems. Serve the spring rolls with Dipping Sauce.

COOK'S FILE

Note: Rice paper wrappers must be kept moist or they become brittle. Continue to sprinkle with cold water while rolling up and if leaving for any length of time before serving.

Place 2 of the prawns side-by-side in the centre and top with the other ingredients.

After folding 2 sides of the wrapper over the top, gently roll up the parcel.

SATAY PRAWNS

Preparation time: 30 minutes
+ marinating
Total cooking time: 20 minutes
Makes 6 skewers

12 raw king prawns (shrimp)
1 clove garlic, crushed
90 g (1/3 cup) smooth peanut
    butter
1 onion, grated
1 tablespoon fish sauce
1/2 teaspoon chilli flakes
1 teaspoon ground turmeric
5 coriander (cilantro) roots,
    chopped
170 ml (2/3 cup) coconut milk

Satay Sauce
2 teaspoons oil
1 teaspoon Red Curry Paste
    (see page 102) or
    commercial paste
1 stem lemon grass (white
    part only), finely chopped
2 teaspoons tamarind purée
250 ml (1 cup) coconut milk
60 g (1/4 cup) smooth peanut
    butter
2 teaspoons sugar
2 teaspoons roasted unsalted
    peanuts, finely chopped

1 Soak six bamboo skewers in water for several hours. Peel the prawns, leaving tails intact; devein.
2 Using a blender or mortar and pestle, blend the garlic, peanut butter, onion, fish sauce, chilli flakes, turmeric, coriander roots and 2 tablespoons of coconut milk until smooth. Stir in the remaining coconut milk.
3 Coat the prawns in the marinade, keeping the tails out if possible. Cover and refrigerate for at least two hours. Thread 2 prawns onto each skewer. Reserve remaining marinade for Satay Sauce, leaving a little to brush over prawns during cooking.
4 To make Satay Sauce: Heat oil in a small pan. Add the curry paste, lemon grass and tamarind, and cook over a high heat for 1 minute or until aromatic. Add the coconut milk, peanut butter and sugar, bring to the boil, reduce heat and simmer, uncov-ered for 2 minutes. Stir in reserved marinade and cook for 2 minutes until well combined and thickened. Serve sprinkled with peanuts.
5 Grill (broil) or barbecue prawns until cooked through, turning once during cooking and brushing with marinade. Serve immediately with Satay Sauce.

COOK'S FILE

Note: If the peanut butter is too thick, thin it with a little water.

Peel the prawns, leaving the tails intact, and then remove the veins.

For Satay Sauce, add the coconut milk, peanut butter and sugar; bring to boil.

During cooking, brush the prawns with the remaining marinade.

THAI FISH CAKES
(Tod Man Pla)

Preparation time: 25 minutes
Total cooking time: 5–10 minutes
Serves 4–6

450 g (1 lb) white fish fillets
3 tablespoons cornflour
    (cornstarch) or rice flour
1 tablespoon fish sauce
1 egg, beaten
15 g (1/2 cup) coriander
    (cilantro) leaves
1–2 teaspoons chopped
    red chillies, optional

3 teaspoons Red Curry Paste
    (see page 102) or
    commercial paste
100 g (3/4 cup) green beans, very
    finely sliced
2 spring onions (scallions),
    finely chopped
125 ml (1/2 cup) oil, for frying
Basic Dipping Sauce
    (see page 100) or
    commercial sauce

1 Process the fish in a food processor for 20 seconds or until smooth. Add the cornflour, fish sauce, beaten egg, coriander leaves, chillies and curry paste. Process for 10 seconds or until well combined.

2 Transfer the fish mixture to a large bowl. Add the green beans and spring onions and mix well. Using wet hands, form two rounded tablespoons of the mixture into a flattish pattie.

3 Heat the oil in a heavy-based frying pan over medium heat. Cook 4 fish cakes at a time until they are dark golden brown on both sides. Drain on paper towels and serve immediately, with a dipping sauce.

COOK'S FILE

Storage time: You can prepare the fish cakes and store them, covered, in the refrigerator for up to four hours.

Add the cornflour, fish sauce, egg, coriander, curry paste and chillies to fish.

Wet your hands and form two rounded tablespoonsful at a time into patties.

After cooking fish cakes until dark golden brown, drain them on paper towels.

STUFFED ZUCCHINI

Preparation time: 30 minutes
Total cooking time: 10 minutes
Makes about 24

4 large zucchini (courgettes)
125 g (4¹/2 oz) minced (ground) pork
50 g (1³/4 oz) peeled raw prawns, (shrimp) very finely chopped
2 cloves garlic, crushed
2 tablespoons coriander (cilantro), finely chopped
¹/2 teaspoon sugar
2 makrut (kaffir) lime leaves, finely chopped, or 1 teaspoon grated lime zest
2 French shallots (eschallots), finely chopped
3 tablespoons coconut cream
2 teaspoons fish sauce
1 tablespoon roasted unsalted peanuts, finely chopped

1 To make filling, cut the zucchini into 4 cm (1¹/2 inch) thick slices. Using a melon baller, scoop out the centre, leaving about 5 mm (¹/4 inch) of flesh on the inside of the skin and on the bottom of each slice. In a bowl, combine the pork, prawn meat, garlic, coriander, sugar, lime leaves, French shallots, 2 tablespoons of the coconut cream and fish sauce.

2 Spoon the filling into the zucchini shells; cover and refrigerate until close to serving time.

3 Place the stuffed zucchini a steamer. Cover and steam for 10 minutes, until the filling is cooked and zucchini are just tender. Serve the zucchini dotted with coconut cream and sprinkled with chopped peanuts.

Scoop out the centre of zucchini slices, leaving a 5 mm (¹/4 inch) shell.

Use two teaspoons to spoon the filling into the zucchini shells.

Steam the stuffed zucchini until they are tender and the filling is cooked.

RED CURRY OYSTERS

Preparation time: 10 minutes
Total cooking time: 5 minutes
Makes 24

2 dozen oysters in half shell
1 tablespoon oil
3 teaspoons Red Curry Paste
  (see page 102) or
  commercial paste

2 cloves garlic, crushed
2 teaspoons grated fresh ginger
1 tablespoon soft brown sugar
2 tablespoons fish sauce
2 makrut (kaffir) lime leaves,
  finely shredded
60 ml (1/4 cup) lime juice

1 Remove the oysters from their shells and wash the shells thoroughly; dry with paper towels and set aside.
2 Heat the oil in a small pan, add curry paste, garlic and ginger; cook over high heat for 1 minute or until aromatic.
3 Add sugar, fish sauce, makrut lime leaves, lime juice and oysters to pan; stir-fry for about 3 minutes or until just cooked. Spoon oysters back into shells for serving. Oysters can be served warm or cold, topped with chopped red chilli.

COOK'S FILE

Hint: For less spicy oysters, reduce curry paste to one or two teaspoons.

Use a teaspoon to remove oysters from their shells. Set oysters aside; wash shells.

Cook the curry paste, garlic and ginger over high heat until aromatic.

Spoon the oysters, with a little of the sauce, into the cleaned shells.

DEEP-FRIED SPRING ROLLS

Preparation time: 35 minutes
Total cooking time: 15 minutes
Makes 25

30 g (1/4 cup) dried rice
    vermicelli
2 cloves garlic
3 coriander (cilantro) roots
1 tablespoon oil
100 g (3 1/2 oz) raw prawn
    (shrimp) meat, finely
    chopped
150 g (5 1/2 oz) lean minced
    (ground) pork
1 medium carrot, grated
3 spring onions (scallions),
    chopped
2 teaspoons fish sauce
1 tablespoon Chilli Sauce
    (see pages 100–101)
    or commercial sauce
2 teaspoons cornflour
    (cornstarch)
2 tablespoons water
25 spring roll wrappers
oil, for deep-frying
Dipping Sauce (see pages
    100–101) or commercial
    sauce, for serving

1 Break the vermicelli into 4 cm (1 1/2 inch) pieces and place the pieces in a heatproof bowl. Cover with boiling water and leave to soak for 4 minutes or until soft; drain well.
2 Chop the garlic and finely chop the coriander roots. Heat the oil in a wok or frying pan. Add the garlic and coriander roots to the wok and stir-fry for 30 seconds. Add the prawn meat and minced pork to the wok and stir-fry for 5 minutes. Use a wooden spoon or fork to break up any lumps. Add the carrot, spring onions, fish sauce, chilli sauce and noodles to the wok. Stir well and then allow to cool.
3 In a small bowl, mix the cornflour and water to form a paste. Place the spring roll wrappers on a damp tea towel and cover with one end of the tea towel.
4 Place 1 spring roll wrapper at a time, with a corner towards you, on another damp tea towel. Using your fingertip, wet all the edges with the cornflour paste.
5 Place 1 tablespoon of filling in the centre of the wrapper and spread the filling out to form a sausage shape. Fold the edges towards the centre and roll up the spring roll tightly. Seal the edge with paste. Continue with the remaining wrappers and filling, keeping the spring rolls covered with a damp tea towel.
6 Heat the oil to moderately hot in a wok or deep frying pan and cook the spring rolls 3 or 4 at a time until they are golden brown. Remove from the oil using a wire mesh strainer, tongs or a slotted spoon. Drain the spring rolls on paper towels and serve immediately with a dipping sauce.

COOK'S FILE

Storage time: Filled spring rolls can be frozen in airtight containers, with freezer wrap between each layer, for up to 3 months. Cook while still frozen. Do not defrost before cooking as they will fall apart.
Hints: Spring roll wrappers are paper-thin and will dry out if you don't place them on a damp tea towel and keep them covered with one end of the tea towel. Defrost frozen ones before use.

Place the vermicelli pieces in a heatproof bowl and cover them with boiling water.

While stir-frying the meat, break up any lumps using a fork or a wooden spoon.

Place the wrappers on a damp tea towel and cover with one end of the tea towel.

Using your fingertip, wet all the edges of the wrapper with the cornflour paste.

Fold the edges of the wrapper towards the centre and then roll up tightly.

Deep-fry the spring rolls 3 or 4 at a time until they are golden.

SON-IN-LAW EGGS

Preparation time: 15 minutes
Total cooking time: 20 minutes
Serves 4

8 eggs
2 tablespoons oil
2 tablespoons soft brown sugar
  or palm sugar
1 tablespoon fish sauce
2 tablespoons tamarind purée

1 teaspoon chopped red chillies,
  optional
15 g (1/2 cup) coriander
  (cilantro) leaves, chopped

1 Place the eggs in a pan of cold water. Bring the water to the boil and cook the eggs for 7 minutes. Drain and run under cold water until cool. Remove the shells.
2 Heat the oil in a wok or frying pan. Add the eggs to the wok in batches and turn frequently over medium heat. When they are golden brown and blistered, remove the eggs from the wok and keep warm.
3 Remove excess oil from pan; add brown sugar, fish sauce, tamarind and chillies. Bring to boil; boil rapidly for 2 minutes or until mixture resembles a syrup. Serve eggs with syrup poured over, sprinkled with coriander leaves.

C O O K ' S   F I L E

Note: The eggs may be boiled up to two days in advance.

Boil the eggs for 7 minutes and then remove the shells.

Use two wooden spoons to turn the eggs frequently until brown and blistered.

Stir the boiling mixture until it resembles a syrup.

CRISP SESAME PRAWNS

Preparation time: 25 minutes +
30 minutes resting
Total cooking time: 15 minutes
Makes 12

30 g (1/4 cup) self-raising flour
2 tablespoons rice flour
2 tablespoons toasted sesame
seeds
1 teaspoon Red Curry Paste
(see page 102) or
commercial paste
1 tablespoon fish sauce
2 teaspoons sesame oil

125 ml (1/2 cup) water
12 raw king prawns (shrimp)
oil, for deep-frying
Chilli Sauce (see pages
100–101) or commercial
sauce, for serving

1 Sift the flours into a medium bowl.
Stir in the sesame seeds. Combine the
curry paste with the fish sauce and
sesame oil in a small jug; add to the
dry ingredients with enough water
to form a batter the consistency of
thick pouring cream. Cover and set
aside for 30 minutes while preparing
the prawns.
2 Peel the prawns leaving tails intact;

devein. Heat the oil to moderately hot
in a deep pan or wok. Holding the
prawns by their tails, dip them into
the batter and then deep-fry, in small
batches, for about 2 minutes or until
golden brown and cooked through.
3 Remove the prawns from the oil
with a wire mesh strainer, slotted
spoon or tongs and then drain on
paper towels. Serve immediately with
some chilli sauce.

COOK'S FILE

Hint: If the oil is too hot, the prawns
will brown quickly before cooking right
through. When tails are pink and
prawns have curled up, they are cooked.

*Add enough water to form batter the
consistency of thick pouring cream.*

*Hold the prawns by their tails and dip
them into the batter before frying.*

*Remove the cooked prawns with a wire
mesh strainer, slotted spoon or tongs.*

GOLDEN PRAWN PUFFS

Preparation time: 15 minutes +
    30 minutes resting
Total cooking time: 5–10 minutes
Serves 4–6

4 medium red chillies
350 g (12 oz) raw prawn
    (shrimp) meat
15 g (½ cup) coriander
    (cilantro) leaves
2 egg whites
1 tablespoon grated ginger
2 cloves garlic, chopped

1 tablespoon fish sauce
60 g (½ cup) rice flour or 40 g
    (⅓ cup) cornflour (cornstarch)
125 ml (½ cup) oil, for frying
Chilli sauce (see pages
    100–101) or commercial
    sauce, for serving

1 Finely chop the red chillies. (Wear rubber gloves to prevent skin irritation.) Place the chillies in a food processor with the prawn meat, coriander leaves, egg whites, ginger, garlic, chillies and fish sauce.
2 Process all the ingredients for 10 seconds or until the mixture is well

combined. Transfer the mixture to a bowl and stir in the flour. Refrigerate the mixture for at least 30 minutes or until you are ready to fry the puffs.
3 Heat the oil in a heavy-based frying pan. Gently drop rounded teaspoons of the mixture into the hot oil. Cook them for 2 minutes, carefully turning with tongs until golden brown on all sides. Drain the puffs on paper towels and serve immediately with chilli sauce. Garnish the puffs with lime wedges and a sprig of coriander.

Wear rubber gloves while holding the chillies to prevent skin irritation.

Process the ingredients briefly until the mixture is well combined.

Gently drop rounded teaspoonsful of the mixture into the hot oil.

FRESH CORN PANCAKES

Preparation time: 20 minutes
Total cooking time: 10–15 minutes
Serves 4–6

2 medium cobs of fresh corn
2 spring onions (scallions),
    finely chopped
2 tablespoons finely chopped
    coriander (cilantro) stems
2 cloves garlic, chopped
2 teaspoons fresh green
    peppercorns, crushed

2 tablespoons cornflour
    (cornstarch)
2 eggs, beaten
1 tablespoon fish sauce
2 teaspoons soft brown sugar
2 tablespoons oil, for frying
Chilli sauce (see pages
    100–101) or commercial
    sauce, for serving

1 Peel the husk from the corn and remove all the fine silk strands. Using a sharp knife, cut downwards along the length of the cobs to remove the kernels; discard the cob.

2 In a bowl, combine the corn, spring onions, coriander, garlic, peppercorns, cornflour, eggs, fish sauce and brown sugar. Beat the mixture, using a wooden spoon, until well combined.
3 Heat the oil in a heavy-based frying pan over medium heat. Drop in tablespoons of the mixture and cook until underside is golden. Turn the pancakes and cook for 30 seconds. Serve immediately with chilli sauce.

C O O K ' S   F I L E

Hint: The thin batter produces a light pancake, so do not add extra flour.

Using a sharp knife, remove all the corn kernels from the cobs.

Place the ingredients in a bowl and beat with a wooden spoon until well combined.

Drop tablespoonsful of mixture in the hot oil and cook until pancakes are golden.

*Golden Prawn Puffs (top) and
Fresh Corn Pancakes*

PORK AND PEANUT DIP

Preparation time: 25 minutes
Total cooking time: 20 minutes
Serves 6–8

1 teaspoon green peppercorns
1 tablespoon oil
2 coriander (cilantro) roots,
    very finely chopped
2 cloves garlic, finely chopped
150 g (5½ oz) fine minced
    (ground) pork
125 ml (½ cup) coconut milk
125 ml (½ cup) water

60 g (¼ cup) crunchy peanut
    butter
1 tablespoon fish sauce
2 teaspoons soft brown sugar
25 g (½ cup) coriander
    (cilantro) leaves, chopped
roasted chopped peanuts
Chilli Sauce (see pages 100–101)
    or commercial sauce
green beans, celery, sugar snap
    peas, spring onions (scallions),
    zucchini (courgette) sticks and
    savoury biscuits for serving

1 Finely crush the peppercorns. Heat the oil in a wok or frying pan.

2 Add the peppercorns, coriander roots and garlic to the wok and stir for 30 seconds over medium heat. Add the pork and stir-fry for 5 minutes, breaking up any lumps of meat. Add coconut milk, water and peanut butter; bring to boil, stirring. Reduce heat; simmer for 10 minutes.

3 Stir in the fish sauce and brown sugar. Pour into a serving bowl and sprinkle with the coriander and peanuts. Drizzle with chilli sauce. Garnish with herbs or strips of chilli, if you like. Serve warm or at room temperature, with vegetable pieces and savoury biscuits for dipping

Finely crush the green peppercorns, using the flat side of the blade of a knife.

Add the minced pork the to wok after cooking the peppercorns, coriander and garlic.

Add the fish sauce and brown sugar to the mixture in the wok and stir.

Separate the lettuce leaves, wash well, pat dry, wrap in a tea towel and refrigerate.

Use a wooden spoon to stir the spring onions and curry paste in the wok.

Add the prawns, coconut milk and chillies to the wok and stir for 3 minutes.

Finally, add the chopped peanuts and stir through the mixture.

SPICY PORK AND PRAWN LETTUCE PARCELS
(Lilies)

Preparation time: 20 minutes +
30 minutes for lettuce crisping
Total cooking time: 8–10 minutes
Serves 4–6

1–2 large lettuces
1 tablespoon oil
3 spring onions (scallions), chopped
2 teaspoons Red Curry Paste (see page 102) or commercial paste
100 g (3¹/₂ oz) lean minced (ground) pork
100 g (3¹/₂ oz) small raw prawns (shrimp), peeled, deveined
1–2 teaspoons chopped red chillies, optional

60 ml (¹/₄ cup) coconut milk
2 teaspoons fish sauce
1 teaspoon soft brown sugar
2 teaspoons grated lime zest
40 g (¹/₄ cup) finely chopped roasted peanuts

1 Separate the lettuce leaves, wash them and pat dry. Wrap them in a dry tea towel. Refrigerate for 30 minutes.
2 Heat oil in a frying pan or wok. Add spring onions and curry paste. Stir for 2 minutes over medium heat.
3 Add the minced pork to the pan and cook, stirring, until browned. Add the prawns, chillies and coconut milk to the pan and stir for 3 minutes.
4 Add fish sauce, brown sugar and lime zest to pan and stir well. Stir in peanuts, allow to cool for 15 minutes. Place a spoonful of mixture on each lettuce leaf until mixture is all used. Parcels can be rolled for easy eating.

COOK'S FILE

Note: The filling must be cooled so that all liquid will be absorbed, making the filling moist and succulent.

MEAT BALLS ON SKEWERS

Preparation time: 25 minutes
Total cooking time: 10 minutes
Serves 4

350 g (12 oz) minced (ground) beef
3 French shallots (eschallots), finely chopped
3 cm (1 1/4 inch) piece ginger, grated
1 tablespoon green or pink peppercorns, crushed
3 cloves garlic, chopped
2 teaspoons soy sauce
2 teaspoons fish sauce
2 teaspoons soft brown sugar
15 g (1/2 cup) coriander (cilantro) leaves
lime wedges
1 cucumber, chopped
3 sliced red or green chillies

1 Chop the minced beef with a cleaver or a large knife until it is very fine. Place the beef, French shallots, ginger, peppercorns, garlic, soy sauce, fish sauce and the brown sugar in a bowl. Mix the ingredients thoroughly until well combined.

2 Using 2 teaspoons of mixture at a time, form into balls. Thread the balls onto the bamboo skewers, using three balls for each skewer.

3 Cook on an oiled grill plate or barbecue. Turn frequently, for about 8 minutes or until the meat is cooked. Sprinkle with coriander. Serve with lime wedges, cucumber and chillies.

COOK'S FILE

Hint: Soak the wooden skewers in water for at least 30 minutes before use, to help prevent them burning.

Use a large, sharp knife or a cleaver to chop the minced beef until very fine.

Form 2 teaspoonsful of mixture at a time into small, compact balls.

Cook the skewered meat balls, turning frequently, for 7–8 minutes.

CHAR-GRILLED BABY OCTOPUS

Preparation time: 1 hour
Total cooking time: 15–25 minutes
Serves 4–6

500 g (1lb 2 oz) baby octopus
2 tablespoons oil
3 cloves garlic, chopped
1 tablespoon green or pink peppercorns
2–4 small red chillies, finely chopped
1 tablespoon fish sauce

1 To clean the octopus, use a small sharp knife to remove the gut by either cutting off the head entirely or by slicing open the head and removing the gut.

2 Pick up the body and use the index finger to push up the beak. Remove the beak and discard. Clean the octopus thoroughly. Cut the head into 2 or 3 pieces. Place the cleaned octopus in a shallow dish.

3 Combine the octopus, oil, garlic, peppercorns and chillies in a bowl; marinate for 30 minutes. Heat a barbecue plate or cast iron pan until very hot. Cook 3 octopus at a time, turning frequently, for 3 minutes or until they turn white. Do not overcook. Sprinkle the fish sauce over the top and serve immediately. These are particularly delicious served with a squeeze of lime. If you wish, you can garnish with a sprig of fresh coriander or some slices of fresh chillies.

COOK'S FILE

Hint: This recipe is also suitable for squid. Wash the tubes, pat them dry and cut them into squares or long strips. Prepare them in the same way as the octopus, making sure you don't overcook, or they will be tough.

Use a sharp knife to slice off the head of the octopus so you can remove the gut.

Use your index finger to push the beak up so you can remove and discard it.

Cook the octopus, turning frequently, until they turn white.

CHICKEN CURRY PUFFS

Preparation time: 1 hour 30 minutes
Total cooking time: 35–45 minutes
Makes about 36

2 tablespoons oil
400 g (14 oz) minced (ground)
    chicken
2 cloves garlic, crushed
1 onion, finely chopped
3 coriander (cilantro) roots,
    finely chopped
2 teaspoons ground turmeric
1¹/2 teaspoons ground cumin
3 teaspoons ground coriander
1 small potato, peeled and
    very finely diced
1 tablespoon chopped coriander
    (cilantro) leaves and stems
3 teaspoons soft brown sugar
¹/2 teaspoon ground
    black pepper
2 small red chillies,
    finely chopped
60 ml (¹/4 cup) fish sauce
1 tablespoon lime juice
oil, extra, for deep-frying
Chilli Sauce (see pages 100–101),
    commercial sauce or Satay
    sauce (see page 12), for
    serving

Pastry
190 g (1¹/2 cups) plain
    (all-purpose) flour
90 g (¹/2 cup) rice flour
¹/2 teaspoon salt
60 g (2¹/4 oz) butter
125 ml (¹/2 cup) coconut milk

1 Heat the oil in a medium wok or pan. Add the chicken and cook over a high heat for 3 minutes or until starting to brown. Break up any lumps as it cooks. Add the crushed garlic, onion, coriander roots, ground turmeric, cumin and coriander, and the potato to the wok; stir-fry over medium heat for about 5 minutes or until potatoes are tender.

2 Add the fresh coriander, sugar, pepper, chillies, fish sauce and lime juice to the wok; stir until well combined and most of the liquid has evaporated; allow to cool.

3 To make Pastry: Sift the flours and salt into a medium bowl and rub in the butter until the mixture is fine and crumbly. Make a well in the centre, add the coconut milk and mix with a knife until the mixture forms a dough. Gently knead until the dough is smooth. Cover with plastic wrap and refrigerate for 30 minutes.

4 Divide the dough into two portions. Roll out one portion on a lightly floured surface until it is about 3 mm (¹/8 inch) thick and then cut into circles with an 8 cm (3 inch) cutter.

5 Place 2 teaspoons of the filling in the centre of each circle, brush the edges of the pastry lightly with water and fold over to enclose the filling; press the edges to seal. Repeat with the remaining half of the dough, re-rolling the scraps until the dough and the filling are all used.

6 Heat the oil in a large wok or pan. Don't put too much oil in the wok—it should be only half full. Deep-fry the puffs, in batches, until puffed and browned. Remove from oil with a wire mesh drainer, slotted spoon or tongs; drain on paper towels. Serve hot with chilli sauce or satay sauce.

COOK'S FILE

Hint: If time is short, substitute the pastry recipe with eight sheets of ready-rolled puff pastry.

Use a spoon or fork to break up any lumps as it cooks.

Stir the ingredients in the wok until well combined and liquid has evaporated.

Add the coconut milk and mix with a knife until it forms a dough.

Cut the rolled out dough into circles, using an 8 cm (3 inch) cutter.

Fold pastry over to enclose the filling and then press the edges to seal.

Add the puffs to the hot oil, cooking only a few at a time.

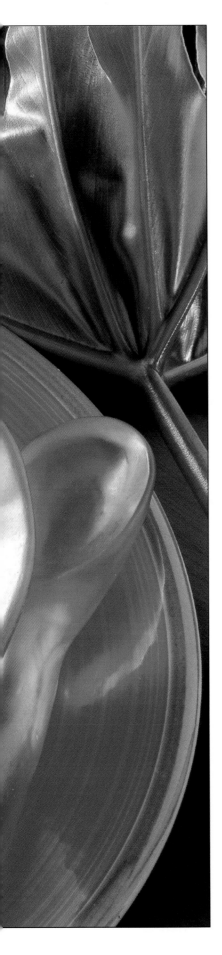

SPICY SOUPS

HOT AND SOUR PRAWN SOUP (Tom Yum Goong)

Preparation time: 25 minutes
Total cooking time: 45 minutes
Serves 4–6

500 g (1 lb 2 oz) raw prawns (shrimp)
1 tablespoon oil
2 litres (8 cups) water
2 tablespoons Red Curry Paste (see page 102) or commercial paste
2 tablespoons tamarind purée
2 teaspoons turmeric
1 teaspoon chopped red chillies
4–6 makrut (kaffir) lime leaves
2 tablespoons fish sauce
2 tablespoons lime juice
2 teaspoons soft brown sugar
7 g (¼ cup) coriander (cilantro) leaves

1 Remove the prawn heads. Peel the prawns, leaving the tails intact. Using a sharp knife, slit each prawn down the back and devein. Set the prawns aside. Heat the oil in a large pan.
2 Add the prawn shells and heads to the pan and cook for 10 minutes over medium–high heat, tossing frequently, until shells and heads are deep orange.
3 Add 250 ml (1 cup) of the water and the curry paste to pan. Boil for 5 minutes, until reduced slightly. Add remaining water and simmer for 20 minutes. Drain, reserving the stock. Discard heads and shells. Return stock to pan.
4 Add the tamarind, turmeric, chillies (optional) and lime leaves to pan; bring to boil and cook for 2 minutes. Add prawns to pan. Cook for 5 minutes or until prawns turn pink. Add the fish sauce, lime juice and sugar to the pan; toss. Serve sprinkled with coriander.

COOK'S FILE

Hint: If tamarind pureé is not available, soak one quarter of a block of tamarind in warm water for 10 minutes. Work the mixture with your fingertips. Remove stones.

Add water and the curry paste to the prawn heads and shells in the pan.

Add the prawns to the spice mixture in pan; bring to the boil and cook.

CHICKEN AND GALANGAL SOUP (Tom Kha Gai)

Preparation time: 20 minutes
Total cooking time: 20 minutes
Serves 4

5 cm (2 inch) piece galangal, peeled and very thinly sliced
500 ml (2 cups) coconut milk
250 ml (1 cup) chicken stock

3 chicken breast fillets, cut into thin strips
1–2 teaspoons finely chopped red chillies
2 tablespoons fish sauce
1 teaspoon soft brown sugar
7 g (¼ cup) coriander (cilantro) leaves

1 Combine the galangal, coconut milk and stock in a medium pan. Bring to the boil and simmer, uncovered, over low heat for 10 minutes, stirring occasionally.

2 Add the chicken and chillies to the pan and simmer for 8 minutes. Add the fish sauce and brown sugar; toss.
3 Add the coriander leaves and serve immediately, garnished with extra sprigs of coriander, if you like.

COOK'S FILE

Hint: You can substitute fresh galangal with five large slices of dried galangal. First soak the slices in one cup of boiling water for 10 minutes before slicing it into small shreds.

Peel the galangal, using a vegetable peeler, and then cut it into thin slices.

Add the chicken strips and the chopped chillies to the pan.

Add the coriander leaves to the soup just before serving.

Place the pumpkin cubes in a bowl and pour half the lime juice over them.

Place the ingredients in a food processor and process until quite smooth.

Simmer the mixture for 10 minutes or until the pumpkin is just tender.

Stir in the basil leaves, remaining lime juice and the fish sauce.

PUMPKIN, PRAWN AND COCONUT SOUP

Preparation time: 15 minutes
Total cooking time: 20 minutes
Serves 4–6

500 g (1 lb 2 oz) pumpkin
4 tablespoons lime juice
8 raw king prawns (shrimp)
2 onions, chopped
1 small red chilli, finely chopped
1 stem lemon grass (white
    part only), chopped
1 teaspoon shrimp paste
1 teaspoon sugar
375 ml (1¹/2 cups) coconut milk
1 teaspoon tamarind purée
250 ml (1 cup) water
125 ml (¹/2 cup) coconut cream
1 tablespoon fish sauce
2 tablespoons Thai basil leaves,
    optional, plus some extra
    leaves or sprigs,
    to garnish

1 Peel pumpkin and scoop out seeds. Cut the pumpkin into cubes and combine with half of the lime juice in a medium bowl. Remove heads from prawns; peel and devein prawns.
2 Process the onions, chilli, lemon grass, shrimp paste, sugar and about 60 ml (¹/4 cup) of the coconut milk, in a food processor until a paste forms.
3 Combine the paste with the remaining coconut milk, tamarind purée and water in a large pan and stir until smooth. Add the pumpkin with the lime juice to the pan; bring to the boil, reduce the heat and simmer, covered, for about 10 minutes or until the pumpkin is just tender.
4 Add the raw prawns and the coconut cream; simmer for 3 minutes or until the prawns are just pink and tender. Stir in the fish sauce, the remaining lime juice and the Thai basil leaves, if using. Pour the soup into warmed bowls and garnish with the extra Thai basil leaves or sprigs.

COOK'S FILE

Note: Thai basil leaves give a distinctive flavour. They are available from Asian specialist food stores.

SEAFOOD SOUP WITH CHILLI AND BASIL

Preparation time: 30–40 minutes
Total cooking time: 30 minutes
Serves 4

8 raw king prawns (shrimp)
8 small black mussels in shells
1 white fish fillet (about 200 g
    or 7 oz)
3 small squid tubes
1 tablespoon oil
1/2 teaspoon ground turmeric
3 stems lemon grass (white
    part only), bruised
2 cm (3/4 inch) piece fresh
    ginger, thinly sliced
8 makrut (kaffir) lime leaves,
    bruised
2 green chillies, chopped
3 coriander (cilantro) roots,
    finely chopped
3 cloves garlic, sliced
3 French shallots (eschallots),
    sliced
2 ripe tomatoes, chopped
750 ml (3 cups) fish stock
2 teaspoons soft brown sugar
2 tablespoons fish sauce
1 tablespoon tamarind purée
1 tablespoon lime juice
15 g (1/4 cup) Thai basil leaves
15 g (1/4 cup) chopped coriander
    (cilantro)
2 small red chillies, chopped

1 Peel prawns, leaving the tails
intact; devein. Remove beards from
mussels and scrub the shells to
remove all the grit.
2 Cut the fish into 4 cm (1 1/2 inch)
pieces. Slit the squid up one side,
score the flesh in a diamond pattern
and cut the squid into pieces.
3 Heat oil in a large pan or wok. Add
turmeric, lemon grass, ginger, lime
leaves, green chillies, coriander, garlic
and shallots. Stir over high heat for
1 minute or until aromatic. Add tomatoes; stir until soft. Add stock to the
pan and bring to boil. Reduce heat and
simmer, covered, for 10 minutes.
4 Add sugar, fish sauce, tamarind and
all the seafood. Bring to the boil, cover,
cook 3–5 minutes until tender. Discard
lemon grass and mussels that have not
opened. Stir through the lime juice and
herbs. Serve sprinkled with red chillies.

*Remove the beards from the mussels and
scrub the shells thoroughly.*

*Use a sharp knife to slit the squid up one
side and score flesh in diamond pattern.*

*Stir the herbs and spices over high heat
for 1 minute or until aromatic.*

*Use tongs to remove the stems of lemon
grass from the soup.*

CORN AND CRAB SOUP WITH CORIANDER

Preparation time: 15 minutes
Total cooking time: 10 minutes
Serves 4

1 1/2 tablespoons oil
6 cloves garlic, chopped
6 French shallots (eschallots), chopped
2 stems lemon grass (white part only), finely chopped

1 tablespoon grated ginger
1 litre (4 cups) chicken stock
250 ml (1 cup) coconut milk
375 g (2 1/2 cups) frozen corn kernels
2 x 170 g (6 oz) cans crab meat, drained
2 tablespoons fish sauce
2 tablespoons lime juice
1 teaspoon soft brown sugar
fresh coriander (cilantro) leaves

1 Heat the oil in a large pan. Add the garlic, shallots, lemon grass and ginger and cook over medium heat for 2 minutes, stirring frequently.

2 Add stock and coconut milk to the pan and bring to the boil. Add the corn and cook for 5 minutes.

3 Add the crab meat, fish sauce, lime juice and brown sugar to the pan and stir. Season and serve immediately, topped with coriander leaves.

COOK'S FILE

Variation: Two eggs, beaten with two tablespoons of water, may be whisked into the soup before serving.

Stir the garlic, French shallots, lemon grass and ginger for 2 minutes.

Add the corn kernels to the pan, stir with a wooden spoon and cook for 5 minutes.

Grind some black pepper into the soup just before serving.

Quick Stir-Fries

CHICKEN, BASIL AND BABY CORN STIR-FRY

Cut 150 g (³/₄ cup) baby corn spears in half vertically. Heat 1 tablespoon of oil in a wok or heavy-based frying pan. In two batches, stir-fry 2 teaspoons of chopped chillies with 4 chicken breast fillets, cut into bite-sized pieces, stirring constantly for 5 minutes, or until the chicken is just cooked. Add the corn, 1 teaspoon of soft brown sugar and 2 tablespoons of fish sauce to the wok; toss well and cover. Cook for 1–2 minutes, or until the corn is just tender. Add 2 tablespoons of lime juice and 30 g (¹/₂ cup) of small basil leaves; toss well and serve immediately with steamed rice. Serves 4

BABY SQUID AND GREEN PEPPERCORN STIR-FRY

In a bowl, combine 500 g (1 lb 2 oz) fresh squid rings, 2 tablespoons of oil and 1 tablespoon of roughly crushed green peppercorns; allow to stand 15 minutes. Heat a large wok or heavy-based frying pan until very hot. Add 2 teaspoons of oil from the marinating squid. Add 4 chopped cloves of garlic and 1 teaspoon of chopped red chillies to the pan and cook for 5 seconds. Add squid to the pan in batches and stir-fry, tossing constantly, for 2 minutes each batch. Transfer each batch to a plate. Reheat wok between each batch. Add 2 tablespoons of fish sauce and 2 teaspoons of soy sauce to wok. When it is bubbling, pour it over the squid and serve immediately, garnished with 30 g (¹/₂ cup) of basil leaves. Accompany with rice. Serves 4

Left to right: Chicken, Basil and Baby Corn Stir-Fry; Baby Squid and Green Peppercorn Stir-Fry; Stir-Fried Beef with Greens; Stir-Fried Chicken with Peanuts and Basil

STIR-FRIED BEEF WITH GREENS

Slice 400 g (14 oz) lean sirloin steak across the grain into thin slices. Heat 1 tablespoon of oil in a wok or large heavy-based frying pan. Add to the pan 4 cloves of chopped garlic, a 5 cm (2 inch) piece of ginger, grated, 2 teaspoons of chopped red chillies and 1 teaspoon freshly ground black pepper; cook for 1 minute. Heat the wok to very hot and add 1 tablespoon of oil. Add the beef in 3 batches and stir-fry each batch for 2 minutes, tossing constantly. Transfer the meat to a plate. Add 2 bunches of baby bok choy (pak choi), cut into short pieces, and some broccoli florets; toss. Cover and steam for 1 minute. Return the meat to the wok; add 2 tablespoons of lime juice and 1 tablespoon of fish sauce. Serve immediately with rice.
Serves 4

STIR-FRIED CHICKEN WITH PEANUTS AND BASIL

Slice 4 chicken breast fillets into small, thin pieces. Combine the chicken and 1 tablespoon of Green Curry Paste (see page 102) or commercial paste, and mix well. Heat 1 tablespoon of oil in a wok or frying pan. Add the chicken to the wok in 2 batches and stir-fry each batch for 3 minutes or until the chicken is cooked through. Transfer to a plate. Add 125 g (4 1/2 oz) of trimmed snow peas (mangetout) to the wok; toss, cover with a lid and steam for 1 minute. Return chicken to the wok; add 2 tablespoons of fish sauce, 1 teaspoon of soft brown sugar, 80 g (1/2 cup) of chopped, roasted peanuts and 30 g (1/2 cup) of small fresh basil leaves; toss gently and serve with steamed rice.
Serves 4

MAIN MEALS

GREEN CHICKEN CURRY

Preparation time: 20 minutes
Total cooking time: 25 minutes
Serves 4

1 tablespoon oil
1 onion, chopped
1–2 tablespoons Green Curry
    Paste (see page 102) or
    commercial paste
375 ml (1¹/₂ cups) coconut milk
125 ml (¹/₂ cup) water
500 g (1 lb 2 oz) chicken thigh
    fillets, cut into bite-sized
    pieces
100 g (³/₄ cup) green beans,
    cut into short pieces
6 makrut (kaffir) lime leaves
1 tablespoon fish sauce
1 tablespoon lime juice
1 teaspoon grated
    lime zest
2 teaspoons soft brown sugar

7 g (¹/₄ cup) coriander (cilantro)
    leaves

1 Heat the oil in a wok or a heavy-based pan. Add onion and curry paste to the wok and cook for about 1 minute, stirring constantly. Add coconut milk and water to the wok. Bring the mixture to the boil.
2 Add the chicken pieces, beans and makrut lime leaves to the wok; stir to combine. Simmer, uncovered, for 15–20 minutes or until the chicken is tender. Add the fish sauce, lime juice and zest, and brown sugar to the wok; stir to combine. Sprinkle with fresh coriander leaves just before serving. Serve with steamed rice.

COOK'S FILE

Note: Chicken thigh fillets are sweet in flavour and a very good texture for curries. You can use breast fillets instead, if you prefer. Do not overcook fillets or they will be tough.

Add the coconut milk and water to the wok and stir with a wooden spoon.

After simmering, stir in the fish sauce, lime juice and zest, and brown sugar.

SWEET RED PORK CURRY WITH CORN AND PEAS

Preparation time: 15 minutes
Total cooking time: 25 minutes
Serves 4

1 tablespoon oil
1–2 tablespoons Red Curry
   Paste (see page 102) or
   commercial paste
500 g (1 lb 2 oz) lean, diced
   pork
250 ml (1 cup) coconut milk
250 ml (1 cup) water
200 g (1 cup) corn kernels or
   150 g (³⁄4 cup) baby corn
   spears
80 g (¹⁄2 cup) green peas
1 tablespoon fish sauce
2 teaspoons soft brown sugar
2 teaspoons grated lime zest
30 g (¹⁄2 cup) shredded Thai
   basil leaves

1 Heat the oil in a wok or heavy-based medium pan. Add the curry paste to the wok and stir for 1 minute. Add the pork and stir-fry, tossing constantly, until the pork browns lightly.
2 Add the coconut milk and water to the wok and bring to the boil. Simmer, uncovered, for 15 minutes.
3 Add the corn and peas to the wok; cook for 5 minutes. Add the fish sauce, brown sugar, lime zest and basil; toss. Garnish with basil leaves, if you like. Serve with steamed rice.

COOK'S FILE

Hint: Remove kernels from 2 fresh corn cobs to make 1 cup.

Add the diced pork to the wok and toss the meat until it turns light brown.

Simmer the mixture in an uncovered wok for 15 minutes.

Stir in the corn and peas and cook the mixture for another 5 minutes.

CHILLI GARLIC QUAIL

Preparation time: 15 minutes
+ marinating
Total cooking time: 15–20 minutes
Serves 4–6

6 quails
1 small red chilli, finely
    chopped
2 tablespoons chopped fresh
    coriander (cilantro) leaves
    and stems
4 cloves garlic, crushed

2 teaspoons soft brown sugar
2 teaspoons Red Curry Paste
    (see page 102) or
    commercial paste
1 tablespoon grated fresh ginger
2 teaspoons light soy sauce
2 teaspoons Chilli Sauce
    (see pages 100–101)
    or commercial sauce
2 teaspoons oil

1 Using poultry shears or kitchen scissors, cut each quail down either side of the backbone and then open out flat. Cut each one in half through the breastbone.

2 Using a mortar and pestle or blender, blend the chilli, coriander leaves and stems, garlic, brown sugar, paste, ginger, soy sauce, chilli sauce and oil, until smooth.

3 Brush the mixture over the quails. Refrigerate in a covered container for at least 2 hours or overnight. Grill (broil) the quails until browned and cooked through, or bake them in a hot oven at 210°C (415°F/Gas 6–7) for 15–20 minutes or until tender. Serve with rice and lime wedges.

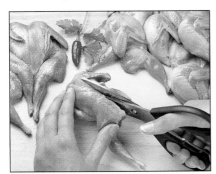

Cut the quails down either side of the backbone and then open out flat.

Blend the ingredients until smooth, using a mortar and pestle or blender.

Use a pastry brush to spread the mixture all over the quails.

CREAMY BEEF AND EGGPLANT CURRY

Preparation time: 20 minutes
Total cooking time: 30–40 minutes
Serves 4

1 tablespoon oil
2–6 teaspoons Red Curry Paste
    (see page 102) or
    commercial paste
500 g (1 lb 2 oz) topside steak, cut
    into strips
375 ml (1½ cups) coconut milk

250 ml (1 cup) water
4 (makrut) kaffir lime leaves
100 g (3½ oz) pea-sized
    eggplants (aubergine) or
    chopped eggplant (aubergine)
1½ tablespoons fish sauce
1½ tablespoons lime juice
2 teaspoons soft brown sugar
30 g (½ cup) Thai basil leaves
    or 15 g (½ cup) coriander
    (cilantro) leaves

1 Heat the oil in a wok. Add the curry paste and stir for 1 minute over medium heat. Add meat in batches

and stir-fry for 3 minutes or until brown. Remove the meat and set it aside.
2 Add coconut milk, water and makrut lime leaves to the wok; bring to the boil and simmer 12 minutes. Add the eggplants to the wok and cook for 5–10 minutes or until tender. Return the beef to the wok and simmer for 3 minutes.
3 Add the fish sauce, lime juice and brown sugar. Add most of the basil or coriander leaves and toss. Serve with steamed rice. Sprinkle with the remaining leaves.

Stir-fry the meat in batches for 3 minutes or until brown; remove and set aside.

Add the eggplants to the wok and bring the mixture to the boil.

Toss the fresh basil or coriander leaves through the curry just before serving.

LOBSTER CURRY WITH CAPSICUM

Preparation time: 25 minutes
Total cooking time: 10–15 minutes
Serves 4–6

2 raw lobster tails
1 tablespoon oil
1–2 tablespoons Red Curry
    Paste (see page 102) or
    commercial paste
2 stems lemon grass
    (white part only), finely
    chopped

1 red capsicum (pepper),
    roughly chopped
250 ml (1 cup) coconut milk
6 dried Chinese dates
1 tablespoon fish sauce
2 teaspoons soft brown sugar
1 teaspoon grated lime zest
15 g (½ cup) coriander
    (cilantro) leaves

1 Cut down the centre of the lobster tails on the underside. Remove the flesh; cut into 2 cm (¾ inch) pieces.
2 Heat the oil in a wok. Add the curry paste and lemon grass and stir for 1 minute over medium heat. Add

lobster pieces a few at a time and stir-fry each batch for 2 minutes, just until golden brown. Transfer each batch of lobster to a plate and set aside.
3 Add capsicum to the wok and stir-fry for 30 seconds. Add coconut milk and dates; bring mixture to the boil and cook for 5 minutes or until dates are plump. Add fish sauce, brown sugar and lime zest. Return the lobster meat to the wok and heat it through. Serve immediately with steamed rice. Sprinkle with coriander leaves.

Use kitchen scissors to cut down centre of the lobster tails on the underside.

Stir-fry the lobster pieces in batches for 2 minutes or until golden brown.

Cook the mixture for about 5 minutes, until the dates are plump.

*Creamy Beef and Eggplant Curry (top) and
Lobster Curry with Capsicum*

BARBECUED GARLIC CHICKEN

Preparation time: 20 minutes +
  marinating
Total cooking time: 10 minutes
Serves 4

6 cloves garlic, crushed
1½ tablespoons cracked
  black peppercorns
30 g (½ cup) chopped fresh
  coriander (cilantro) leaves
  and stems
4 coriander (cilantro) roots,
  chopped
80 ml (⅓ cup) lime juice
1 teaspoon soft brown sugar
1 teaspoon ground turmeric
2 teaspoons light soy sauce
4 chicken breast fillets

Cucumber and Tomato Salad
1 small green cucumber, unpeeled
1 large egg tomato
¼ small red onion, sliced thinly
1 small red or green chilli,
  finely chopped
2 tablespoons coriander
  (cilantro) leaves
2 tablespoons lime juice
1 teaspoon soft brown sugar
1 tablespoon fish sauce

1 Using a mortar and pestle or blender, blend the garlic, peppercorns, coriander, lime juice, sugar, turmeric and soy sauce until smooth. Transfer to a bowl.
2 Remove tenderloins from the fillets. Score the top surface of each fillet three times. Add fillets and tenderloins to marinade; cover. Refrigerate for 2 hours minimum, turning occasionally.
3 To make Salad: Halve the cucumber and scoop out the seeds with a teaspoon. Cut into slices. Halve the tomato lengthways and slice.
4 Combine cucumber, tomato, onion, chilli and coriander. Drizzle with the combined lime juice, sugar and fish sauce. Cook the chicken on a lightly greased barbecue hotplate for 3 minutes each side or until tender. The tenderloins need less time to cook. Serve with the salad.

COOK'S FILE

Hint: The same marinade can be used for fish fillets, quails or lamb cutlets.

Add the chopped coriander roots to the other ingredients and blend until smooth.

Separate the tenderloins from the chicken fillets by pulling them away.

Use a teaspoon to scoop the seeds out of the halved cucumber.

Drizzle the combined lime juice, sugar and fish sauce over the salad ingredients.

Roast all the whole chillies in a hot wok or large pan until they begin to brown.

Bruise lemon grass and coriander roots by crushing them with flat side of a knife.

Add the fish pieces to the mixture in the wok and simmer gently for 2–3 minutes.

Just before serving, stir in the green chillies, fish sauce, salt and lime juice.

FISH FILLETS IN COCONUT MILK

Preparation time: 10 minutes
Total cooking time: 15 minutes
Serves 4

2 long green chillies
2 small red chillies
400 g (14 oz) white fish fillets
2 stems lemon grass
2 coriander (cilantro) roots
4 makrut (kaffir) lime leaves, plus extra, for garnish
2 cm (3/4 inch) piece fresh ginger, thinly sliced
2 cloves garlic, crushed
3 green onions, white part only, finely sliced
1 teaspoon soft brown sugar
250 ml (1 cup) coconut milk
125 ml (1/2 cup) coconut cream
1 tablespoon fish sauce
salt
2–3 tablespoons lime juice

1 Heat a wok or large pan until hot; add the whole chillies and roast until just beginning to brown all over. Remove the green chillies from the wok, cool and slice. Cut the fish into 5 cm (2 inch) pieces.
2 Bruise the lemon grass and coriander roots by crushing them with the flat side of a knife.
3 Add lemon grass, coriander roots, lime leaves, ginger, garlic, onions, sugar and coconut milk to the wok. Stir it to combine; bring to the boil. Reduce heat and simmer, uncovered, for 2 minutes. Add the fish pieces and simmer gently for 2–3 minutes or until the fish is tender. Stir in the coconut cream.
4 Stir through the chopped green chillies, fish sauce, and salt and lime juice, to taste. Garnish with some whole lime leaves, if you like.

HOT PORK CURRY WITH PUMPKIN

Preparation time: 20 minutes
Total cooking time: 25 minutes
Serves 4

1 tablespoon oil
1–2 tablespoons Red Curry
    Paste (see page 102) or
    commercial paste
500 g (1 lb 2 oz) lean pork, cut
    into thick strips or chunks
250 ml (1 cup) coconut milk
125 ml (½ cup) water

350 g (12 oz) butternut
    pumpkin (squash) or
    Japanese pumpkin, peeled
    and cut into small chunks
6 makrut (kaffir) lime leaves
60 ml (¼ cup) coconut cream
1 tablespoon fish sauce
1 teaspoon soft brown sugar
2 red chillies, thinly sliced

1 Heat the oil in a wok or heavy-based pan. Add the curry paste and stir for 1 minute.
2 Add the pork to the wok and stir-fry over medium-high heat until golden brown. Add the coconut milk, water, pumpkin and lime leaves to wok; reduce heat and simmer for 18 minutes or until the pork is tender.
3 Add coconut cream, fish sauce and brown sugar to the wok and stir to combine. Scatter sliced chilli over the top. Serve with steamed rice. Garnish with sprigs of basil, if you like.

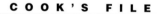
COOK'S FILE

Note: Butternut and Japanese pumpkins are tender, sweet varieties—they are a bright orange colour.

Add the curry paste to the hot oil and stir with a wooden spoon for 1 minute.

Add the pork pieces to the wok and stir-fry over medium heat until golden brown.

Add the coconut cream, fish sauce and brown sugar to the wok and stir well.

FISH CUTLETS IN RED SAUCE

Preparation time: 10 minutes
Total cooking time: 35 minutes
Serves 4

1 tablespoon oil
2 onions, finely chopped
4 ripe tomatoes, peeled
    and chopped
60 ml (¼ cup) water
1 tablespoon sambal oelek
1 tablespoon soft brown sugar
4 blue-eyed cod cutlets or
    other firm fish cutlets

2 tablespoons fish sauce
2 tablespoons rice vinegar
    or white vinegar
2 tablespooons chopped
    coriander (cilantro)

1 Heat the oil in a wok or large frying pan and add the onions. Cook over medium heat for 2 minutes or until soft but not browned. Add the chopped tomatoes, water, sambal oelek and brown sugar to the wok. Bring to the boil; reduce heat and simmer, covered, for 20–25 minutes or until the sauce is thick.

2 Add the fish cutlets to the wok and spoon some sauce over them. Cover the wok and cook the fish for 3–5 minutes and then gently turn to cook the other side. If the wok or pan is too small to cook all the fish cutlets at once, cook them in two batches.

3 Transfer the fish to serving plates. Add the fish sauce, vinegar and chopped coriander to the sauce in the wok and then stir well before spooning the sauce over the fish. Serve with steamed rice.

COOK'S FILE

Note: Skin can be removed from the fish cutlets before cooking, if you prefer. Fish cooks quickly so have everything prepared before you start.

Add the chopped tomatoes, water, sambal oelek and brown sugar to the wok.

Place fish cutlets in the wok, in batches if necessary, and spoon some sauce over.

Transfer fish to serving plates and add fish sauce, vinegar and coriander to wok.

CHICKEN AND PEANUT PANANG CURRY

Preparation time: 25 minutes
Total cooking time: 30–40 minutes
Serves 4

1 tablespoon oil
1 large red onion, chopped
1–2 tablespoons Panang Curry
   Paste (see page 103) or
   commercial paste
250 ml (1 cup) coconut milk
500 g (1 lb 2 oz) chicken thigh
   fillets, cut in bite-sized pieces

4 makrut (kaffir) lime leaves
60 ml (¼ cup) coconut cream
1 tablespoon fish sauce
1 tablespoon lime juice
2 teaspoons soft brown sugar
80 g (½ cup) roasted peanuts,
   chopped
30 g (½ cup) Thai basil leaves
80 g (½ cup) chopped pineapple
1 cucumber, sliced
Chilli Sauce (see pages
   100–101) or commercial
   sauce, for serving, optional

1 Heat the oil in a wok or large frying pan. Add the onion and curry paste to the wok and stir over medium heat for 2 minutes. Add the coconut milk and bring to the boil.
2 Add the chicken and kaffir lime leaves to the wok; reduce heat and cook for 15 minutes. Remove chicken with a wire mesh strainer or slotted spoon. Simmer the sauce for 5 minutes or until it is reduced and quite thick.
3 Return the chicken to the wok. Add the coconut cream, fish sauce, lime juice and sugar; cook for 5 minutes. Stir in the peanuts, basil and pineapple. Serve with sliced cucumber on the side, some chilli sauce, if desired, as well as steamed rice.

Add the red onion and curry paste to the hot oil and stir with a wooden spoon.

Remove the cooked chicken from the wok and set it aside while cooking the sauce.

Stir in the pineapple, basil leaves and chopped peanuts just before serving.

STEAMED FISH IN BANANA LEAVES

Preparation time: 45 minutes
Total cooking time: 7–10 minutes
Makes 10

2 large banana leaves
350 g (12 oz) white fish fillets
1–2 tablespoons Red Curry
  Paste (see page 102) or
  commercial paste
250 ml (1 cup) coconut cream
150 g (2 cups) finely shredded
  cabbage

2 tablespoons fish sauce
2 tablespoons lime juice
1–2 tablespoons Chilli Sauce
  (see pages 100–101) or
  commercial sauce
1 fresh red chilli, chopped,
  optional

1 Cut the banana leaves into squares 10 x 10 cm (4 x 4 inch). Make a 3 cm (1¹/₄ inch) cut towards the centre on each corner. Fold in the corners; staple and/or tie around with string to form a cup; trim corners if necessary.
2 Cut fish into thin strips and place in a bowl with the curry paste and

coconut cream; stir gently to combine. Place spoonfuls of the fish mixture in the centre of each banana leaf cup.
3 Line a large steaming basket with extra banana leaves or cabbage leaves. Place the prepared cups in the basket. Top fish with shredded cabbage and a little fish sauce. Place the basket over a wok of simmering water; cover and steam for approximately 7 minutes. Drizzle with lime juice and chilli sauce; serve immediately, topped with chilli.

COOK'S FILE

Hint: The parcels can be cooked in foil squares instead of banana leaves.

Fold in the cut corners and then staple them and/or tie around edge with string.

Fill each cup almost to the top with fish mixture. Leave room for the cabbage.

Place shredded cabbage over the top. Add a little fish sauce before steaming.

BRAISED BEEF WITH SPINACH AND LEEKS

Preparation time: 10 minutes + marinating
Total cooking time: 25 minutes
Serves 4

400 g (14 oz) beef fillet
2 tablespoons light soy sauce
2 tablespoons fish sauce
3 tablespoons oil
4 coriander (cilantro) roots, finely chopped
15 g (1/4 cup) chopped coriander (cilantro) leaves and stems
2 cloves garlic, crushed

2 teaspoons cracked black peppercorns
1 tablespoon soft brown sugar
250 ml (1/2 cup) water
1 leek, sliced
20 English spinach leaves, stalks removed
60 ml (1/4 cup) lime juice

1 Cut the beef into 2.5 cm (1 inch) thick pieces and place in a bowl. Place the sauces, 1 tablespoon oil, coriander, garlic, peppercorns and brown sugar in blender; blend until smooth. Pour marinade over beef; cover and refrigerate for at least 2 hours, or overnight.
2 Drain the beef, reserving the marinade. Heat 1 tablespoon of the oil in a wok or large frying pan. Fry the pieces, browning well on each side. Add reserved marinade and water. Reduce heat; simmer for 8 minutes. Remove the meat; keep warm, simmer sauce for 10 minutes and set aside. Slice beef into large bite-sized pieces.
3 Heat remaining oil in a wok; add leek and stir-fry over medium heat for 2 minutes. Add spinach and cook for 30 seconds or until softened. Arrange with the slices of meat; pour sauce over steak. Drizzle with lime juice; serve. Garnish with chilli slices .

COOK'S FILE

Variation: Use rump steak instead of fillet—buy a thick slice and trim off fat.

Place the pieces of beef in a bowl and pour the marinade over the top.

Brown the steaks on each side in a wok or heavy-based pan.

Add the spinach to the leek and toss it for about 30 seconds until softened.

FRIED CRISPY CHICKEN

Preparation time: 20 minutes + marinating
Total cooking time: 30 minutes
Serves 4

4 chicken Marylands (leg quarters) or 8 drumsticks
4 cloves garlic, chopped
3 coriander (cilantro) roots, finely chopped

2 teaspoons ground turmeric
1 teaspoon freshly ground pepper
1 teaspoon salt
1 teaspoon caster (superfine) sugar
2 tablespoons Chilli Sauce (see pages 100–101) or commercial sauce, plus extra, for serving, optional

1 Boil the chicken in a pan of water for 15 minutes or until it is cooked through; allow to cool completely.

2 Process the garlic, coriander root, turmeric, pepper, salt, sugar and chilli sauce in a food processor or grind in a mortar and pestle until smooth.
3 Brush paste over chicken; cover, refrigerate for 30 minutes. Heat some oil in a heavy-based pan; add chicken, cook until dark brown, turning frequently. Drain on paper towels. Serve hot or cold with chilli sauce, if desired.

Chicken juice should run clear, not pink, when the chicken is cooked.

Grind or process the ingredients until the mixture is smooth.

Use a pastry brush to spread the ground paste all over the chicken pieces.

Braised Beef with Spinach and Leeks (top) and Fried Crispy Chicken

GREEN PRAWN CURRY

Preparation time: 35 minutes
Total cooking time: 25 minutes
Serves 4

500 g (1 lb 2 oz) raw prawns
   (shrimp)
375 ml (1½ cups) coconut milk
250 ml (1 cup) water
1–3 tablespoons Green Curry
   Paste (see page 102) or
   commercial paste

6 makrut (kaffir) lime leaves
100 g (3½ oz) green snake
   beans, cut in short pieces,
   optional
2 tablespoons fish sauce
2 tablespoons lime juice
2 teaspoons grated
   lime zest
2 teaspoons soft brown sugar
30 g (1 cup) fresh coriander
   (cilantro) leaves

1 Peel the prawns, leaving the tails intact. Devein and set aside.

2 Heat the coconut milk and water in a wok or pan over medium heat for 5 minutes. Add the curry paste, makrut lime leaves and beans to the wok. Bring to the boil; simmer for 10 minutes.

3 Add prawns to the wok; simmer for 5–6 minutes or until prawns are pink. Add the fish sauce, lime juice and zest and brown sugar. Taste the sauce and adjust the seasonings if necessary. Serve sprinkled with coriander leaves. Serve with steamed rice.

Peel the prawns, leaving the tails intact and then remove veins from the backs.

Add makrut lime leaves with curry paste and pieces of snake beans to the wok.

When prawns are cooked, add fish sauce, lime juice and zest, and sugar to the wok.

Hold one end of the squid, pull the skin away from the flesh and discard it.

Remove the frying pan from the heat; stir in the minced meat, fish sauce and flour.

CHAR-GRILLED STUFFED SQUID TUBES

Preparation time: 30 minutes
Total cooking time: 6–10 minutes
Serves 4

8 very small squid
2 tablespoons oil
4 cloves garlic, chopped
2 stems lemon grass, (white part only) finely chopped
4 coriander (cilantro) roots, chopped
1–2 teaspoons Green Curry Paste (see page 102) or commercial paste
125 g (4½ oz) minced (ground) pork
100 g (3½ oz) minced (ground) chicken
2 tablespoons fish sauce
2 tablespoons rice flour
1 tablespoon soy sauce
1 tablespoon water
2 teaspoons soft brown sugar
Chilli Sauce (see pages 100–101) or commercial sauce, for serving

1 To prepare the squid, pull the tentacles from the body of the squid. Using your fingers, pull quill from pouch of the squid. Pull the skin away from the flesh and discard it. Wash the tubes thoroughly.

2 Heat half the oil in a frying pan over medium heat. Add the garlic, lemon grass, coriander root and the curry paste to the pan; stir-fry for 2 minutes. Remove from heat; add the minced pork, minced chicken, the fish sauce and rice flour to pan. Mix together well.

3 Fill each tube with the mixture and secure the end with a toothpick. In a bowl, combine the soy sauce, water and sugar; brush this mixture over the squid tubes.

4 Brush a barbecue flatplate with the remaining oil; heat until the flatplate is very hot. Add the tubes and cook, turning frequently, for 4–6 minutes or until the tube is just firm to the touch. Leave for 2 minutes before slicing, or serve whole. Serve with chilli sauce and steamed rice.

COOK'S FILE

Note: Don't use pre-cleaned squid as

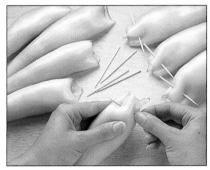

Secure the ends of the filled squid tubes with toothpicks.

Leave the cooked tubes for 2 minutes before slicing, or serve them whole.

the tip will have been removed during cleaning and the stuffing will come out during cooking.

PRAWN OMELETTE

Preparation time: 15 minutes
Total cooking time: 15 minutes
Serves 2–4

2 tablespoons oil
3 cloves garlic, chopped
2 stems lemon grass (white part only), finely chopped
2 coriander (cilantro) roots, finely chopped
1–2 teaspoons chopped red chillies
500 g (1 lb 2 oz) small raw prawns (shrimp), shelled
3 spring onions (scallions), chopped, plus 15 g (¼ cup) shredded, to garnish
½ teaspoon black pepper

1 tablespoon fish sauce
2 teaspoons soft brown sugar
4 eggs
2 tablespoons water
2 teaspoons fish sauce
coriander (cilantro) sprigs, to garnish
Chilli Sauce (see pages 100–101) or commercial sauce, for serving

1 Heat half the oil in a large wok or heavy-based pan. Add garlic, lemon grass, coriander root and chillies to wok and stir over medium heat for 20 seconds. Add prawns to wok and stir-fry until prawns change colour. Add chopped spring onions, pepper, fish sauce and brown sugar to the wok; toss well and remove from wok.

2 Beat the eggs, water and fish sauce in a bowl until mixture is foamy. Add remaining oil to wok and swirl around to coat the sides. Heat the wok and, when it is very hot, pour in the egg mixture and swirl the mixture around the wok. Allow the mixture to set on the underneath edges, frequently lifting the edges once set, and tilting the wok a little to let the unset mixture run underneath. Repeat this process until the omelette is nearly all set.

3 Place three-quarters of the prawn mixture in the centre of the omelette and fold in sides of the omelette to form a square, overlapping the sides a little, or simply fold omelette in half. Slide omelette onto a serving plate and place remaining prawn mixture on the top. Sprinkle with the shredded spring onions. Garnish with coriander; serve with chilli sauce and steamed rice.

Add the chopped spring onions, brown sugar, pepper and fish sauce to wok; toss.

Tilt the wok and lift edges of the omelette to let the unset mixture run underneath.

Fold the sides of the omelette over the mixture to form a square.

GINGER CHICKEN WITH BLACK FUNGUS

Preparation time: 25 minutes
Total cooking time: 15 minutes
Serves 4

3 tablespoons black (wood)
   fungus
1 tablespoon oil
3 cloves garlic, chopped
6 cm (2½ inch) ginger, cut into
   fine shreds
500 g (1 lb 2 oz) chicken breast
   fillets, sliced

4 spring onions (scallions),
   chopped
1 tablespoon soy sauce
1 tablespoon fish sauce
2 teaspoons brown sugar
½ red capsicum (pepper), finely
   sliced
15 g (½ cup) coriander
   (cilantro) leaves
30 g (½ cup) shredded Thai
   basil leaves

1 Place the fungus in a bowl of hot water for 15 minutes until it is soft and swollen; drain and chop roughly.
2 Heat oil in a large wok; add garlic and ginger and stir-fry for 1 minute. Cook the chicken in batches; stir-fry over high heat until chicken changes colour. Return all the chicken to the wok. Add spring onions and soy sauce; stir-fry for 1 minute.
3 Add the fish sauce, brown sugar and fungus. Stir thoroughly; cover and steam for 2 minutes. Serve scattered with red capsicum, coriander and basil, with steamed rice.

COOK'S FILE

Note: Black (wood) fungus is a dried mushroom that swells to many times its size when soaked in hot water

When fungus is soft and swollen, drain it well and chop it with a sharp knife.

Add the spring onions and soy sauce; stir-fry for a minute.

Cover the wok and allow the mixture to steam for 2 minutes.

PRAWNS IN SOURED LIME COCONUT SAUCE

Preparation time: 20 minutes
Total cooking time: 30 minutes
Serves 4

1 teaspoon shrimp paste
250 ml (1 cup) coconut milk
250 ml (1 cup) water
2 stems lemon grass (white part only), finely chopped
2–4 makrut (kaffir) lime leaves
2 teaspoons chopped red chillies
2 tablespoons tamarind purée
2 teaspoons fish sauce

1 teaspoon soft brown sugar
500 g (1 lb 2 oz) raw prawns (shrimp)
15 g (1/4 cup) shredded coconut, toasted
zest of 2 fresh limes

1 Place the shrimp paste on a small piece of foil; fold one side over and then fold into a parcel. Cook the parcel under a hot grill (broiler) for 2 minutes on each side.
2 Combine coconut milk and water in a wok or frying pan and cook over medium heat until just boiling. Add lemon grass, makrut lime leaves and chillies to wok; reduce heat; simmer for

7 minutes. Add the tamarind purée, fish sauce, shrimp paste and brown sugar to the wok and simmer for 8 minutes.
3 Peel the prawns, leaving the tails intact. Cut down the backs of the prawns and devein. Add the prawns to the sauce and cook for 5 minutes or until the prawns turn pink. Sprinkle with coconut and long, thin shreds of toasted lime zest just before serving with steamed rice.

COOK'S FILE

Notes: Prawns can be cooked and served in their shells. Provide a finger bowl and napkin for each person.

Place the shrimp paste on a small piece of foil and then fold to make a parcel.

Stir in the lemon grass, chillies and lime leaves; reduce heat and simmer.

Add the prepared prawns to the mixture and cook until the prawns turn pink.

CRISP PRAWNS AND SCALLOPS WITH RED CURRY

Preparation time: 25 minutes
+ 30 minutes refrigeration
Total cooking time: 10 minutes
Serves 4

500 g (1 lb 2 oz) raw prawns (shrimp), peeled and deveined, with the tails left intact
250 g (9 oz) fresh scallops

1–2 tablespoons Red Curry Paste (see page 102) or commercial paste
2 tablespoons oil
2 medium ripe tomatoes, chopped
2 tablespoons lime juice
2 teaspoons finely grated lime zest, to garnish

1 Combine the prawns, scallops, curry paste and oil in a bowl; cover with plastic wrap and refrigerate for about 30 minutes.

2 Heat a wok or heavy-based frying pan until it is very hot. Toss the seafood in the curry paste again to coat well and add to the wok in 2–3 batches; cook each batch for 3 minutes, tossing frequently.

3 Remove from the heat; return all the seafood to the wok. Add the tomatoes and lime juice and stir well. Serve immediately, garnished with lime zest. Serve with steamed rice.

COOK'S FILE

Note: Cook seafood quickly in a hot wok to seal in the juices and flavour and prevent it becoming tough.

Place the prawns, scallops, oil and curry paste in a bowl and toss to combine well.

Toss the seafood in a hot wok, in batches, for 3 minutes each batch.

Add the chopped tomatoes and lime juice to the seafood and toss to combine.

STEAMED FISH CUTLETS WITH GINGER AND CHILLI

Preparation time: 15 minutes
Total cooking time: 10 minutes
Serves 4

4 medium-sized snapper or
   other firm white fish cutlets
5 cm (2 inch) piece fresh ginger,
   cut into fine shreds
2 cloves garlic, chopped
2 teaspoons chopped red
   chillies

2 tablespoons finely chopped
   coriander (cilantro) stalks
3 spring onions (scallions), cut
   into fine 4 cm (1¼ inch) long
   shreds
2 tablespoons lime juice
lime wedges, for serving

1 Line a bamboo steaming basket
with banana leaves or baking paper.
(The steaming basket is lined for this
dish so that the fish will not stick or
taste of bamboo.)
2 Arrange the fish cutlets in the base
of the basket and top with the ginger,
garlic, chillies and coriander stalks.

Cover and steam over a wok or large
pan of boiling water for 5–6 minutes.
3 Remove the lid and sprinkle the
spring onions and lime juice over the
fish. Cover the basket and steam for
30 seconds, or until the fish is cooked.
Serve immediately with wedges of
lime and steamed rice that has been
garnished with onions or herbs.

COOK'S FILE

Variation: A small, whole fish may
be used instead of cutlets. Cut three
deep slashes into the thickest part of
the flesh and steam for 15 minutes.

*Line the bamboo steaming basket with
banana leaves or baking paper.*

*Top the fish with ginger, garlic, chillies
and coriander stalks before steaming.*

*The fish is cooked when the flesh flakes
easily with a fork.*

CORIANDER PORK WITH FRESH PINEAPPLE

Preparation time: 25 minutes
Total cooking time: 10–12 minutes
Serves 4

400 g (14 oz) pork loin or fillet
¼ medium pineapple
1 tablespoon oil
4 cloves garlic, chopped
4 spring onions (scallions),
   chopped
1 tablespoon fish sauce

1 tablespoon lime juice
15 g (½ cup) coriander
   (cilantro) leaves
15 g (¼ cup) chopped mint

1 Cut the pork into thin slices, using
a very sharp knife.
2 Trim the skin from the pineapple
and cut the flesh into small bite-sized
pieces. Heat the oil in a wok or heavy-
based frying pan, add the garlic and
spring onions and cook for 1 minute.
Remove from the wok.
3 Heat the wok to very hot; add the
pork in 2 or 3 batches and stir-fry

each batch for 3 minutes or until the
meat is just cooked. Return the meat,
garlic and onions to the wok and then
add the pineapple pieces, fish sauce
and lime juice. Toss well. Just before
serving, sprinkle with the coriander
leaves and chopped mint; toss lightly.
Serve with rice.

COOK'S FILE

Hints: To make the meat easier to
slice, freeze it until it is just firm and
slice thinly while still frozen.
• Do not overcook the pork or it will
become tough.

*Use a sharp knife to cut the pork into
thin slices.*

*Slice the skin from the pineapple and cut
the flesh into small, bite-sized pieces.*

*Stir-fry each batch of pork for 3 minutes
or until just cooked.*

*Steamed Fish Cutlets with Ginger and Chilli (top)
and Coriander Pork with Fresh Pineapple*

CRISP FRIED WHOLE FISH WITH SOUR PEPPER AND CORIANDER SAUCE

Preparation time: 20 minutes
Total cooking time: 15 minutes
Serves 4

1 kg (2 lb 4 oz) whole snapper
    or red emperor (or any firm
    sweet fish), scaled
    and cleaned
250 ml (1 cup) oil, for frying
4 spring onions (scallions),
    chopped
5 cm (2 inch) piece fresh ginger,
    grated
2–4 teaspoons fresh green
    peppercorns, crushed
2 teaspoons chopped red
    chillies
125 ml (½ cup) coconut milk
1 tablespoon tamarind purée
1 tablespoon fish sauce
30 g (1 cup) fresh coriander
    (cilantro) leaves
Chilli Sauce (see pages
    100–101) or commercial
    sauce, for serving

1 Cut a shallow, criss-cross pattern on both sides of the fish. Using kitchen scissors, or a sharp knife, trim any long fins. Heat the oil in a large wok or heavy-based, deep frying pan.
2 Place the whole fish in the oil and cook for 4–5 minutes on each side, moving fish around in the oil to ensure the whole fish is crisp and cooked (including the tail and head). Drain fish well on paper towels; place on a warmed serving plate and keep warm.
3 Drain almost all the oil from the wok, heat over medium heat, add the spring onions, ginger, peppercorns and chillies; stir-fry for 3 minutes. Add coconut milk, tamarind and fish sauce to the wok. Cook for 2 minutes.
4 Spread the sauce over the fish; sprinkle with coriander leaves and then serve, on a bed of lettuce if you like, with chilli sauce.

COOK'S FILE

Note: For serving, use tongs or a small spatula to lift pieces of fish away from the bones. Then remove the bones, or turn fish over, and lift pieces of fish from the underside.

Cut a criss-cross pattern on both sides of the fish, using a sharp knife.

Move the fish around the wok to ensure the whole fish is crisp and cooked.

Stir-fry the spring onions, peppercorns, ginger and chillies for 3 minutes.

Spread the sauce all over the fish and garnish with coriander before serving.

STEAMED MUSSELS WITH LEMON GRASS, BASIL AND WINE

Preparation time: 30 minutes
Total cooking time: 15 minutes
Serves 4–6

1 kg (2 lb 4 oz) mussels
1 tablespoon oil
1 medium onion, chopped
4 cloves garlic, chopped
2 stems lemon grass (white part only), chopped
1–2 teaspoons chopped red chillies
250 ml (1 cup) white wine or water
1 tablespoon fish sauce
60 g (1 cup) fresh Thai basil leaves, roughly chopped

1 Scrub the outside of the mussels with a brush. Remove and discard the beards. Soak the mussels in a bowl of cold water for 10 minutes; drain and discard any open shells.

2 Heat the oil in a wok or large pan. Add the onion, garlic, lemon grass and chillies, and cook for 4 minutes over low heat, stirring occasionally. Add the wine and fish sauce to the wok and cook for 3 minutes.

3 Add the mussels to the wok and toss well. Cover the wok; increase the heat and cook for 3–4 minutes or until mussels open. Discard any unopened mussels. Add the chopped basil and toss well. Serve with steamed rice.

COOK'S FILE

Hint: Do not overcook the mussels or they will become tough. Use small black fresh mussels.

After scrubbing the mussels with a brush, pull the beards off and discard.

Add the wine and fish sauce to the wok and cook for 3 minutes.

If any mussels have not opened during cooking, discard them.

59

MUSAMAN BEEF CURRY

Preparation time: 25 minutes
Total cooking time: 50 minutes
Serves 4

1 tablespoon oil
500 g (1 lb 2 oz) topside, cut
  into large cubes
1–2 tablespoons Musaman
  Curry Paste (see page 103)
  or commercial paste
2 large onions, cut into wedges
  or thick slices
2 large potatoes, peeled
  and diced
375 ml (1¹/2 cups) coconut milk
250 ml (1 cup) water
2 cardamom pods
2 bay leaves
2 tablespoons tamarind purée
2 teaspoons soft brown sugar
80 g (¹/2 cup) peanuts, roasted,
  optional
2 red chillies, finely sliced

1 Heat the oil in a wok or large heavy-based pan. Add the meat to the wok in batches and stir-fry each batch over medium heat until it is well browned. Remove the meat from the wok and set aside on paper towels. Add the curry paste to the wok and stir for 1 minute.
2 Add the onions and diced potatoes to the wok and cook, stirring often until golden brown. Remove from the wok and set aside.
3 Add the coconut milk and water. Bring to the boil, stirring; reduce heat and simmer for 15 minutes, uncovered. Return the meat, onions and potatoes to the wok.
4 Add the cardamom, bay leaves, tamarind purée and sugar. Stir well and then simmer, uncovered, for 20 minutes or until the meat is tender. Remove the bay leaves from the mixture. Add the peanuts, if you're using them. When ready to serve, scatter the sliced red chillies over the top. Serve with steamed rice.

COOK'S FILE

Hints: If tamarind purée is not available, soak a 2 cm (³/4 inch) block of pulp with 60 ml (¹/4 cup) of hot water. Work with your fingertips until pulpy. Remove the seeds before use.

Remove the browned meat from the wok and place on paper towels.

Add the sliced onions and diced potatoes to the curry paste and stir until brown.

Return the meat, onions and potatoes to the wok.

When the meat is cooked, remove the bay leaves from curry with a fork or tongs.

FISH FILLETS WITH CHILLI LIME SAUCE

Preparation time: 10 minutes
Total cooking time: 10 minutes
Serves 4–6

45 g (1/4 cup) rice flour or
   30 g (1/4 cup) cornflour
   (cornstarch)
6 medium-sized firm white fish
   fillets, such as perch, bream
   or flake
2 tablespoons oil

Chilli Lime Sauce
6 cloves garlic, crushed
2 teaspoons chopped red
   chillies
1 tablespoon soft brown sugar
60 ml (1/4 cup) lime juice
2 teaspoons finely grated
   lime zest
2 tablespoons water

1 Place the flour on a plate and press the fish fillets lightly in the flour until coated. Shake off excess flour.
2 Heat the oil in a heavy-based frying pan. Add fillets in batches to the pan and cook them over medium heat,

turning once. Remove to a warmed serving plate and keep warm.
3 To make Chilli Lime Sauce: Drain excess oil from pan; add garlic and chillies and cook for 2 minutes, stirring constantly. Add sugar, juice and zest, and water. Bring sauce to the boil, stirring. Cook for 1 minute; spoon over the fish. Serve with rice.

COOK'S FILE

Hints: Remove the seeds from the chillies if you want to make the sauce less hot.
• Two tablespoons of coconut cream can be added to the sauce, if you like.

Press the fish fillets lightly in the flour to coat well. Shake off any excess flour.

Only turn the fish fillets once during cooking. Transfer to a warmed plate.

Stir in the brown sugar, lime juice and zest, and water.

SPICY BEEF CURRY

Preparation time: 20 minutes
Total cooking time: 30–35 minutes
Serves 4

1 tablespoon oil
1 large onion, chopped
1–2 tablespoons Green Curry
  Paste (see page 102) or
  commercial paste
500 g (1 lb 2 oz) round or blade
  steak, cut into thick strips
185 ml (³/4 cup) coconut milk
60 ml (¹/4 cup) water
6 makrut (kaffir) lime leaves
100 g (3¹/2 oz) pea-sized
  eggplants (aubergines)
2 tablespoons fish sauce
1 teaspoon soft brown sugar
2 teaspoons finely grated
  lime zest
15 g (¹/2 cup) fresh coriander
  (cilantro) leaves
30 g (¹/2 cup) shredded basil
  leaves

1 Heat the oil in a wok or large frying pan. Add the onion and curry paste, and stir for 2 minutes over medium heat until fragrant.

2 Heat the wok until it is very hot; add beef in 2 batches and stir-fry until brown. Return all meat to pan. Add coconut milk, water and lime leaves to wok. Bring to the boil, reduce heat and simmer for 10 minutes. Add the eggplants and simmer, uncovered, for another 10 minutes or until both the beef and eggplants are tender.

3 Add the fish sauce, brown sugar and lime zest to wok and mix well. Stir in the coriander and basil. Serve immediately with steamed rice.

Stir curry paste and onion over medium heat for 2 minutes or until fragrant.

After simmering for 10 minutes, add the eggplants to the wok.

Stir in the coriander leaves and shredded basil just before serving.

SCALLOPS AND FISH IN GINGER AND LIME

Preparation time: 15 minutes
Total cooking time: 12–15 minutes
Serves 4

500 g (1 lb 2 oz) firm white fish
   fillets
350 g (12 oz) scallops
2 tablespoons oil
5 cm (2 inch) piece fresh ginger,
   grated
3 spring onions (scallions),
   chopped

1 tablespoon lime juice
2 tablespoons chilli jam
2 tablespoons water
2 teaspoons finely grated
   lime zest
7 g (1/4 cup) fresh coriander
   (cilantro) leaves
lime wedges, optional

1 Cut the fish into bite-sized pieces and remove any black veins from the scallops. Heat half the oil in a wok or large frying pan. Add the ginger and spring onions and cook for 30 seconds. Remove from the wok and set aside. Reheat the wok and when it is very

hot, add the remaining oil.
2 Add the fish and scallops in 3 batches and stir-fry for 2–3 minutes. Remove from the wok and set aside.
3 Add the lime juice, chilli jam, water and lime zest to the wok; bring to the boil, stirring. Return the fish, scallops, and onion/ginger mixture to the wok, tossing gently with the sauce. Serve immediately sprinkled with coriander leaves. Garnish with lime wedges and serve the seafood with steamed rice.

COOK'S FILE

Hint: Refrigerate the chilli jam after opening.

Remove any of the large black veins from the scallops.

Remove the fish and scallops from the wok with a wooden spoon or tongs.

Toss the seafood gently through the sauce, using a wooden spoon.

NOODLES & RICE

THAI FRIED NOODLES (Phad Thai)

Preparation time: 25 minutes
Total cooking time: 10–15 minutes
Serves 4

250 g (9 oz) thick rice stick
   noodles
2 tablespoons oil
3 cloves garlic, chopped
2 teaspoons chopped red chillies
150 g (5½ oz) pork, thinly
   sliced
100 g (3½ oz) peeled raw prawn
   (shrimp) meat chopped
½ bunch garlic chives,
   chopped
2 tablespoons fish sauce
2 tablespoons lime juice
2 teaspoons soft brown
   sugar
2 eggs, beaten

90 g (1 cup) bean sprouts
sprigs of coriander (cilantro)
40 g (¼ cup) roasted peanuts,
   chopped

1 Soak the rice stick noodles in warm water for 10 minutes or until they are soft. Drain and set aside. Heat the oil in a wok or large frying pan. When the oil is very hot, add the garlic, chillies and pork; stir constantly for 2 minutes.
2 Add the prawn meat to the wok. Cook, stirring constantly, for 3 minutes. Add the garlic chives and drained noodles to the wok; cover and cook for another minute.
3 Add the fish sauce, lime juice, sugar and eggs to the wok. Toss well with tongs or two wooden spoons until heated through.
4 Sprinkle with sprouts, coriander and peanuts. Traditionally served with crisp fried onion, soft brown sugar and chopped peanuts on the side.

After stir-frying the pork for 2 minutes, stir in the prawn meat.

Toss the ingredients, using tongs or two wooden spoons, until heated through.

FRIED CRISPY NOODLES (Mee Grob)

Preparation time: 30 minutes
Total cooking time: 20 minutes
Serves 4

100 g (1 cup) rice vermicelli
50 ml (2 cups) oil, for frying
100 g (3¹/2 oz) fried bean curd
(tofu), cut into matchsticks
2 cloves garlic, finely chopped
4 cm (1¹/2 inch) piece of ginger,
grated
150 g (5¹/2 oz) minced (ground)
chicken or pork, or a
combination of both
100g (3¹/2 oz) raw prawn
(shrimp) meat, finely
chopped
1 tablespoon white vinegar
2 tablespoons fish sauce
2 tablespoons soft brown sugar
2 tablespoons Chilli Sauce
(see pages 100–101) or
commercial sauce
1 teaspoon chopped red
chillies
2 small knobs pickled
garlic, chopped
¹/4 bunch fresh garlic
chives, chopped
30 g (1 cup) fresh coriander
(cilantro) leaves

1 Place the vermicelli in a bowl of hot water for 1 minute; drain and allow to dry for 20 minutes. Heat oil in a wok or deep pan; add the bean curd in 2 batches and cook for 1 minute or until golden and crisp. Drain.

2 Add the completely dry vermicelli to wok in several batches; cook 10 seconds or until puffed and crisp. Remove from the oil immediately to prevent the vermicelli absorbing too much oil. Drain on paper towels; cool.

3 Drain all but 1 tablespoon of the oil from the wok. Reheat wok over high heat and add the garlic, ginger, minced meat and prawn meat; stir-fry for 2 minutes or until golden brown. Add the vin-egar, fish sauce, brown sugar, chilli sauce and chillies; stir until boiling.

4 Just before serving, add the noodles and bean curd to the wok and toss thoroughly. Quickly toss through the pickled garlic, chives and coriander.

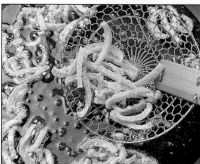

Cook bean curd for 1 minute until golden brown. Remove with wire mesh strainer.

Add the vermicelli to the wok in batches and cook until puffed and crisp.

Add the chopped garlic, grated ginger, mince and prawn meat to the wok.

Just before serving, return the noodles and bean curd to the wok, and toss.

CHIANG MAI NOODLES

Preparation time: 20 minutes
Total cooking time: 15 minutes
Serves 4

3 Asian or French shallots
    (eschallots)
500 g (1 lb 2 oz) egg noodles
1 tablespoon oil
6 cloves garlic, chopped
2 teaspoons finely chopped
    red chillies, optional
1–2 tablespoons Red Curry
    Paste (see page 102) or
    commercial paste

350 g (12 oz) lean chicken or
    pork, finely sliced
1 carrot, cut into fine,
    thin strips
2 tablespoons fish sauce
2 teaspoons soft brown sugar
3 spring onions (scallions),
    finely sliced
7 g (¼ cup) coriander (cilantro)
    leaves
Basic Dipping Sauce (see
    page 100), for serving

1 Peel and chop the shallots.
2 Cook the noodles in a wok or
pan of rapidly boiling water for
2–3 minutes until they are just tender.

Drain the noodles and keep them
warm. Heat the oil in a wok or large
frying pan until it is very hot. Add the
shallots, garlic, chillies and curry
paste; stir-fry for 2 minutes or until
fragrant. Add the chicken or pork to
the wok in 2 batches and cook
for 3 minutes or until the meat
changes colour.
3 Return all the meat to the wok. Add
carrot, fish sauce and brown sugar to
the wok; bring to boil. Divide noodles
between serving bowls and mix in
portions of the chicken mixture and
spring onions. Top with coriander
leaves. Serve immediately with Basic
Dipping Sauce.

*Use a sharp knife to peel and finely chop
the shallots.*

*Cook the noodles in a wok or pan of
rapidly boiling water until just tender.*

*Place all the meat back into the wok. Add
carrot, fish sauce and brown sugar.*

STEAMED RICE

Preparation time: 5 minutes
Total cooking time: 12–15 minutes
Serves 4–6

500 g (2¹/₂ cups) jasmine rice
a few drops of oil

1 Place the rice in a fine strainer and wash it thoroughly under cold, running water until the water runs clear.

Wash the rice thoroughly under cold, running water.

2 Place the rice in a heavy-based pan. Add enough cold water to come about 3 cm (1¹/₄ inches) above the rice. Add the oil to the pan and bring water to a gentle boil over a medium heat.
3 Boil until the water is level with the rice and tunnels or bubbles appear; cover pan. Turn heat as low as possible; cook for 10 minutes, shaking the pan from time to time. Remove pan from the heat and set aside for 5 minutes before serving. Rice in the picture is topped with garlic chives.

Add a few drops of oil to the pan to help prevent the grains sticking together.

COOK'S FILE

Hint: As a general rule with jasmine rice, the ratio is two cups of washed rice to three cups of water. One cup of uncooked rice yields three cups of rice after cooking. Washing the rice removes excess starch—this helps to keep the grains separate when cooked. Adding oil to the water also assists in keeping the grains separate. When cooking rice by the absorption method, don't stir during cooking and don't remove the lid.

Boil until tunnels or bubbles appear; cover the pan and cook for 10 minutes.

FRIED NOODLES WITH MUSHROOMS AND BARBECUED PORK

Preparation time: 30 minutes
Total cooking time: 6 minutes
Serves 4

8 dried Chinese mushrooms
2 tablespoons oil
4 cloves garlic, chopped
4 cm (1¹/₂ inch) ginger, grated
1–2 teaspoons chopped
    red chillies
100 g (3¹/₂ oz) barbecued pork,
    cut into small pieces
200 g (7 oz) egg noodles

2 teaspoons fish sauce
2 tablespoons lime juice
2 teaspoons soft brown sugar
2 tablespoons crisp fried garlic
    (see Glossary)
2 tablespoons crisp fried onion
    (see Glossary)
chilli flakes

1 Soak the mushrooms in hot water for 20 minutes. Drain and cut them into quarters.
2 Heat the oil in a large wok or frying pan. Add the garlic, ginger and chillies and stir-fry for 1 minute over high heat. Add the pork to the wok and stir for 1 minute.
3 Add the egg noodles and the

mushrooms, toss well. Sprinkle the fish sauce, lime juice and soft brown sugar over the pork and then toss quickly; cover and steam for 30 seconds. Sprinkle the fried garlic and onions, and chilli flakes over the top. You can garnish with strips of the green section of spring onions.

COOK'S FILE

Hints: This dish is quite salty so serve it with a selection of milder flavoured dishes.
• Garnish with fresh coriander (cilantro) leaves or sprigs of Thai basil.

Drain the Chinese mushrooms and use a sharp knife to cut them into quarters.

Add the pork pieces to the wok and stir with a wooden spoon for a minute.

Cover the wok and allow the noodles to steam for 30 seconds.

Steamed Rice (top) and Fried Noodles with Mushrooms and Barbecued Pork

FRIED RICE WITH DRIED SHRIMP

Preparation time: 25 minutes
Total cooking time: 20 minutes
Serves 4

3 tablespoons oil
1 egg, beaten with 2 teaspoons water
2 cloves garlic, chopped
3 spring onions (scallions), chopped
6 tablespoons dried shrimp, roughly chopped
740 g (4 cups) cold steamed rice

(see page 68)
1 tablespoon fish sauce
2 teaspoons soy sauce
30 g (1 cup) coriander (cilantro) leaves
1/4 pineapple, cut into pieces
1 medium cucumber (any type), cut into pieces
Chilli Sauce (see pages 100–101) or commercial sauce, optional, for serving

1 Heat 1 tablespoon of oil in a wok or large frying pan. Pour in the egg mixture and swirl the wok until the egg mixture sets. Cut into quarters, flip each quarter and cook the other side. Remove cooked egg from the wok and cut into thin strips.

2 Add the remaining oil, reheat the wok and add the garlic, spring onions and shrimp; stir for 2 minutes. Add the rice to the wok, stir-fry for 5 minutes over high heat tossing constantly until the rice is heated through.

3 Add the sauces, coriander and omelette strips to wok. Toss well. Arrange the rice on a serving platter. Serve with combined pineapple and cucumber, and chilli sauce, if desired.

COOK'S FILE

Note: Rice should be refrigerated overnight before making fried rice.

Cut the omelette into quarters to make it easy to turn over and cook the other side.

Stir-fry the garlic, spring onions and shrimp for 2 minutes.

Just before serving, add the sauces, coriander and omelette strips to wok; toss.

Cut the fried bean curd into small cubes, using a sharp knife.

Place the vermicelli noodles in a heatproof bowl and pour boiling water over them.

VEGETARIAN RICE NOODLES

Preparation time: 25 minutes
Total cooking time: 5–7 minutes
Serves 4–6

100 g (3¹/2 oz) fried bean curd
    (tofu)
8 dried Chinese mushrooms
250 g (2¹/2 cups) rice vermicelli
2 tablespoons oil
3 cloves garlic, chopped
4 cm (1¹/2 inch) piece of ginger,
    grated
1 medium carrot, peeled
    and cut into thin shreds
100 g (3¹/2 oz) green beans,
    cut into short lengths
¹/2 red capsicum (pepper),
    cut into fine strips
2 tablespoons soy sauce
1 tablespoon fish sauce
2 teaspoons soft brown sugar
100 g (1 cup) bean sprouts,
    plus a handful extra,
    to garnish

75 g (1 cup) finely shredded
    cabbage
Chilli Sauce (see pages
    100–101) or commercial
    sauce, for serving

1 Cut bean curd into small cubes. Soak dried Chinese mushrooms in hot water for 20 minutes. Drain and slice.
2 In a heatproof bowl, pour boiling water over the vermicelli and soak them for 1–4 minutes until soft; drain.
3 Heat a wok or large heavy-based frying pan. Add the oil and, when very hot, add the garlic, ginger and bean curd; stir-fry 1 minute. Add carrot, beans, capsicum strips and mushrooms to the wok; stir-fry for 2 minutes. Add the sauces and sugar; toss well, cover and steam for 1 minute.
4 Add the vermicelli, bean sprouts and all but a few tablespoonsful of cabbage; toss, cover and steam for 30 seconds. Arrange noodles on a serving platter, garnish with bean sprouts and remaining cabbage and serve with chilli sauce.

Stir-fry the garlic, ginger and bean curd in the hot oil for 1 minute.

Add vermicelli, bean sprouts and cabbage to wok; toss well and steam for 1 minute.

COOK'S FILE

Note: Traditionally, the scraggly ends of the bean sprouts are pinched off. It is worth the extra effort.

FRIED RICE WITH CORIANDER AND BASIL

Preparation time: 20 minutes +
 overnight standing
Total cooking time: 20 minutes
Serves 4

465 g (2^1/$_2$ cups) jasmine rice
100 g (3^1/$_2$ oz) pork loin
2 tablespoons oil
3 cm (1^1/$_4$ inch) piece of pork
 fat, chopped
4 cloves garlic, chopped
4 cm (1^1/$_2$ inch) piece of grated
 ginger
2 teaspoons chopped red chillies
2 chicken thigh fillets, diced
1 tablespoon fish sauce
2 teaspoons soy sauce
2 spring onions (scallions),
 chopped
60 g (1 cup) Thai basil leaves,
 chopped
15 g (^{1}/$_2$ cup) coriander
 (cilantro) leaves, chopped,
 reserving some for garnish

1 Steam the jasmine rice. Allow to cool and then refrigerate overnight.
2 Dice the pork loin. Heat the oil in a wok or large heavy-based frying pan. When oil is very hot, add pork fat, garlic, ginger and chillies; stir 2 minutes.
3 Add diced chicken and pork to wok and stir-fry for 3 minutes or until it changes colour. Break up lumps in the rice. Add rice to wok; toss well with two wooden spoons. Warm the rice, add sauces and toss through spring onions and herbs. Serve immediately.

Cut the pork loin into small dice, using a sharp knife.

Add the pork fat, garlic, ginger and chillies to wok and stir.

Break up any lumps in the cold rice. Add to wok; toss, using two wooden spoons.

CURRIED RICE NOODLES WITH CHICKEN

Preparation time: 25 minutes
Total cooking time: 10–15 minutes
Serves 4–6

200 g (7 oz) thick rice stick
noodles
1½ tablespoons oil
1 tablespoon Red Curry Paste
(see page 102) or
commercial paste
3 chicken thigh fillets, cut into
fine strips
1 teaspoon chopped red chillies

2 tablespoons fish sauce
2 tablespoons lime juice
100 g (1 cup) bean sprouts
80 g (½ cup) roasted chopped
peanuts
20 g (¼ cup) crisp fried onion
(see Glossary)
25 g (¼ cup) crisp fried garlic
(see Glossary)
30 g (1 cup) coriander (cilantro)
leaves

1 Cook the noodles in a pot of rapidly boiling water for 2 minutes; drain. Toss the noodles with 2 teaspoons of oil to prevent strands sticking together; set aside.

2 Heat the remaining oil in a wok; add the curry paste and stir for 1 minute or until fragrant. Add the chicken in batches and stir-fry for 2 minutes or until golden brown. Return all the chicken to the pan.

3 Add chillies, fish sauce and lime juice; bring to the boil and simmer for 1 minute. Add the bean sprouts and noodles and toss well. Arrange the noodles on a plate and sprinkle with peanuts, onions, garlic and coriander leaves. Serve immediately.

COOK'S FILE

Note: Rice stick noodles are flat and are available from Asian food stores.

Toss 2 teaspoons of oil through the noodles, using 2 wooden spoons.

Cook each batch of chicken for 2 minutes and return all the chicken to the pan.

Add the bean sprouts and noodles to the wok and toss well to distribute evenly.

PINEAPPLE FRIED RICE

Preparation time: 25 minutes
Total cooking time: 15 minutes
Serves 6–8

1 medium ripe pineapple
60 ml (1/4 cup) oil
3 cloves garlic, chopped
1 medium onion, chopped
1–2 teaspoons chopped
    red chillies
150 g (5½ oz) pork loin, cut
    into very small dice
150 g (5½ oz) raw prawn
    (shrimp) meat
555 g (3 cups) cold steamed rice
    (see page 68),
2 tablespoons finely chopped
    fresh Thai basil
2 tablespoons fish sauce
3 spring onions (scallions),
    finely sliced
2 tablespoons chopped
    coriander (cilantro) leaves
fresh red or green chillies,
    sliced

1 Cut the pineapple in half lengthways. Run a knife around the edge of the pineapple and then cut and scoop out the flesh. Chop into small pieces, discarding core, and set aside.
2 Heat 1 tablespoon of oil in a wok or large frying pan over high heat. Add the garlic, onion and chillies to the wok and cook for 1 minute. Add the pork; stir-fry, tossing constantly, for 2 minutes. Add the prawn meat to the wok and cook, stirring, for another 3 minutes. Remove all the meat from the wok and set aside. Reheat the wok and stir-fry the pineapple pieces for 3 minutes or until heated through and lightly golden; remove from the wok.
3 Add the remaining oil to the wok. When the oil is very hot, add the rice and stir-fry for 2 minutes, tossing constantly. Return the pork, prawns and pineapple to the wok and stir thoroughly. Remove wok from heat.
4 Add the basil and fish sauce, and toss well. Fill the pineapple shells with the fried rice. Scatter spring onions, coriander and chillies over the top and serve immediately.

Run a sharp knife around the inside edge of the pineapple before removing flesh.

Add the the garlic, onion and chillies to the wok and stir for 1 minute.

Return the pork, prawns and pineapple to the wok and stir thoroughly.

For serving, fill the pineapple shells with the fried rice.

PORK BALL CURRY WITH EGG NOODLES

Preparation time: 15 minutes
Total cooking time: 20 minutes
Serves 4

200 g (7 oz) minced (ground)
    pork
3 cloves garlic, chopped
2 stems lemon grass (white part
    only), finely chopped
3 cm (1¼ inch) piece ginger,
    grated
1 tablespoon oil
1–2 tablespoons Green Curry
    Paste (see page 102)
    or commercial paste

375 ml (1½ cups) coconut milk
250 ml (1 cup) water
2 tablespoons fish sauce
2 teaspoons soft brown sugar
30 g (½ cup) chopped Thai
    basil leaves
200 g (7 oz) fresh egg noodles
3 spring onions (scallions),
    sliced
fresh coriander (cilantro) leaves
2 red or green chillies, sliced

1 Finely chop the minced pork with a cleaver or large knife. Combine the pork, garlic, lemon grass and ginger in a bowl and mix thoroughly. Form teaspoonsful into small balls.
2 Heat the oil in a wok or frying pan, add the curry paste and cook over low heat, stirring constantly, for 1 minute or until fragrant. Add the coconut milk and water to the wok. Stir until boiling; reduce heat and simmer, uncovered, for 5 minutes. Add pork balls. Gently cook for 5 minutes or until cooked. Add fish sauce, sugar and chopped basil.
3 Cook the noodles in boiling water for 4 minutes or until tender, and drain. Place the noodles on serving plates, add the pork balls and curry sauce; toss well and then serve. Scatter spring onions, coriander leaves and chillies over the top.

COOK'S FILE

Hint: Serve this dish quickly as the noodles soak up sauce on standing.

Form teaspoonsful of the pork mixture into small balls.

Add the coconut milk and water to the wok and stir until boiling.

Add the noodles to rapidly boiling water and cook for 4 minutes.

SALADS & VEGETABLES

CHICKEN AND VEGETABLE SALAD

Preparation time: 30 minutes
Total cooking time: 20 minutes
Serves 4–6

2 chicken breast fillets
250 ml (1 cup) water
3 slices fresh ginger
2 stems lemon grass (white
    part only), roughly chopped
2 tablespoons fish sauce
250 g (9 oz) broccoli florets
150 g (3/4 cup) baby corn spears
100 g (31/2 oz) snow peas
    (mangetout), trimmed
1 red capsicum (pepper), cut
    into strips
3 spring onions (scallions), cut
    into strips
125 ml (1/2 cup) Chilli Sauce
    (see pages 100–101)
    or commercial sauce
2 tablespoons honey or
    2 tablespoons palm sugar
    mixed with a little
    warm water

2 tablespoons lime juice
2 teaspoons grated lime zest
60 ml (1/4 cup) coriander
    (cilantro) leaves

1 Slice chicken into short, thin strips. Place the water, ginger, lemon grass and the fish sauce in a frying pan. Bring to the boil and simmer for 5 minutes.
2 Add the chicken to the pan and cook in the hot liquid for 5 minutes, stirring occasionally until the chicken turns white and is cooked. Drain and allow to cool. Discard liquid.
3 Bring a large pan of water to the boil. Cook the broccoli, corn, snow peas, capsicum and spring onions for 2 minutes. Drain and plunge into ice-cold water. Drain.
4 Combine the chilli sauce, honey, lime juice and zest in a small bowl and mix well. Arrange the vegetables and chicken on a serving platter. Pour the sauce over the top and gently toss. Sprinkle with coriander leaves. cauliflower florets or carrots.

Cook the chicken in the hot liquid until it turns white and is cooked through.

In a small bowl, mix the chilli sauce, honey, lime juice and zest.

STIR-FRIED VEGETABLES

Preparation time: 25 minutes
Total cooking time: 5 minutes
Serves 4

1 bunch asparagus, ends
   snapped off
1 tablespoon oil
4 cloves garlic, chopped
3 stems lemon grass (white part
   only), finely chopped
2 teaspoons chopped red chilli
2 sticks celery, cut into
   3 cm (1¼ inch) pieces

100 g (3½ oz) green beans, cut
   into 3 cm (1¼ inch) pieces
½ red capsicum (pepper), cut
   into thin 3 cm (1¼ inch)
   pieces
1–2 tablespoons fish sauce
1–2 tablespoons Chilli Sauce
   (see pages 100–101)
   or commercial sauce, or
   chopped fresh chillies
1 teaspoon soy sauce
100 g (3½ oz) bean sprouts
40 g (¼ cup) roasted chopped
   peanuts, optional
7 g (¼ cup) coriander (cilantro)
   leaves, optional

1 Cut the asparagus into 3 cm
(1¼ inch) pieces. Heat the oil in a wok
or large frying pan. Add the garlic and
lemon grass to the wok and cook for
1 minute.
2 Add the chillies, celery and beans;
stir-fry for 1 minute. Add asparagus
and capsicum to wok; toss well, cover
and steam 1 minute.
3 Add the sauces to the wok and toss
well. Add bean sprouts; toss again.
Serve with peanuts and coriander
leaves scattered over the top.

*Cut the asparagus into 3 cm (1¼ inch)
pieces. Cut all vegetables a similar size.*

*Stir the chilli, celery and beans into the
mixture for about a minute.*

*Add sauces to wok and toss well, using a
wooden spoon, until evenly distributed.*

Soak the dried shrimp in the hot water for about 15 minutes, until plump.

Add the sliced garlic to the hot oil and fry until browned and crisp.

Blend sugar, juice, peppercorns, coriander, crushed garlic and fish sauce until smooth.

Add half of the fried garlic to bowl with the other ingredients; mix with dressing.

RED CABBAGE SALAD

Preparation time: 45 minutes
Total cooking time: 3 minutes
Serves 4–6

1 medium onion, finely
   sliced
1 teaspoon salt
2 tablespoons dried shrimp
1 tablespoon oil
6 cloves garlic, sliced
150 g (2 cups) finely shredded
   red cabbage
150 g (2 cups) finely shredded
   Chinese cabbage or
   curly white cabbage
40 g (1/4 cup) roasted unsalted
   peanuts, chopped

Dressing
2 teaspoons soft brown sugar
2 tablespoons lime juice
1/2 teaspoon cracked
   black peppercorns

2 tablespoons chopped fresh
   coriander (cilantro) leaves
   and stems
3 cloves garlic, crushed
1 tablespoon fish sauce

1 Combine the sliced onion and salt in a colander. Set aside for 30 minutes; rinse and drain well. Meanwhile, place the shrimp in a heatproof bowl; cover with hot water and soak for 15 minutes; drain and chop finely.

2 Heat the oil in a small pan. Add the garlic and fry until browned and crisp; drain on paper towels.

3 To make Dressing: Place the sugar, lime juice, peppercorns, coriander, crushed garlic and fish sauce in a blender and blend until smooth.

4 Combine the onion, shrimp and half the fried garlic with the shredded cabbages, in a large bowl. Pour the dressing over the top and mix well. Serve sprinkled with the remaining fried garlic and peanuts. Garnish with fresh coriander, if you wish.

COOK'S FILE

Note: Use a large, flat-bladed knife or cleaver to shred the cabbage. Cut it into manageable portions first.

GREEN PAWPAW AND PEANUT SALAD

Preparation time: 25 minutes
Total cooking time: 5 minutes
Serves 4–6

50 g (1³/4 oz) dried shrimp
100 g (3¹/2 oz) green beans, cut
  into short pieces
1 medium lettuce
¹/2 medium green pawpaw,
  peeled and grated
60 ml (¹/4 cup) lime juice

2 tablespoons fish sauce
2 teaspoons soft brown sugar
1–2 teaspoons chopped fresh
  red chillies
80 g (¹/2 cup) roasted peanuts,
  chopped
1 red chilli, finely diced

1 Pound the dried shrimp in a mortar and pestle, or chop finely.
2 Cook the beans in a pan of boiling water for 2 minutes. Drain and then plunge into iced water; drain again. Shred the lettuce and arrange on a serving plate. Top with the beans,

shrimp mixture and pawpaw.
3 Combine the lime juice, fish sauce, brown sugar and chillies in a small bowl; mix well. Pour over the salad and spread peanuts and chillies over the top.

COOK'S FILE

Note: Green pawpaw and dried shrimp are available at Asian food speciality stores. There are no substitutes for these ingredients.
Hints: When grating pawpaw, lightly oil your hands or wear gloves. Pawpaw can be very sticky and hard to wash off.

Pound the dried shrimp in a mortar and pestle until finely ground.

Place the cooked beans into a strainer and plunge into a bowl of iced water.

Mix the lime juice, fish sauce, brown sugar and chillies in a small bowl.

Turn the eggplants until the skin begins to char, making sure to cook all sides.

Blend the chillies, garlic, coriander roots, onion, sugar, lime juice and fish sauce.

Stir the paste over high heat for 1 minute, or until fragrant.

Add half the basil leaves and the tofu to the wok. Stir gently until mixed.

SPICY ROASTED EGGPLANT WITH TOFU

Preparation time: 15 minutes
Total cooking time: 10–15 minutes
Serves 4

4 small lady-finger eggplants
   (aubergines), 400 g (14 oz)
250 g (9 oz) silken tofu or soft
   bean curd
2–4 small fresh red or green
   chillies
4 cloves garlic, crushed
4 coriander (cilantro) roots,
   chopped
1 small brown onion, chopped
3 teaspoons soft brown sugar
2 tablespoons lime juice
2 tablespoons fish sauce
1 tablespoon oil
30 g (1/2 cup) Thai basil leaves
2 teaspoons dried shrimp,
   finely chopped, optional

1 Heat a medium frying pan or wok until hot, add the eggplant, cook until the skin begins to char, turning to cook all sides. Remove from the heat, cool. Slice eggplant diagonally into 2 cm (3/4 inch) thick slices. Drain tofu and cut into 3 cm (1 1/4 inch) cubes.
2 Using a food processor or a blender, blend the chillies, garlic, coriander roots, onion, sugar, lime juice and fish sauce until smooth.
3 Heat the oil in the same pan or wok, add the paste and stir over high heat for 1 minute or until fragrant. Add the eggplant, stir to combine and cook, covered, for 3 minutes or until just tender.
4 Add half the basil leaves and the tofu and gently stir through. Serve garnished with remaining basil leaves and dried shrimp, if desired.

COOK'S FILE

Notes: If you prefer a milder, less spicy dish, use only two chillies.

• This dish can be eaten hot or as a cold accompaniment.
• Tofu is available fresh or in long-life packs.

81

STIR-FRIED CAULIFLOWER AND SNAKE BEANS

Preparation time: 10 minutes
Total cooking time: 10 minutes
Serves 4

4 coriander (cilantro) roots,
    chopped, or 1 tablespoon
    chopped leaves and stems
1 teaspoon soft brown sugar
1/2 teaspoon ground turmeric
2 cloves garlic, crushed
2 tablespoons fish sauce
400 g (14 oz) cauliflower
6 spring onions (scallions),
    reserving some green, for
    garnish
200 g (7 oz) snake beans
2 tablespoons oil
4 cloves garlic, extra, sliced
    lengthways
20 leaves English spinach,
    coarsely shredded
1/2 teaspoon cracked
    black pepper
125 ml (1/2 cup) water
1 tablespoon lime juice

1 Using a mortar and pestle or a blender, blend the coriander, sugar, turmeric, crushed garlic and 1 tablespoon fish sauce to make a smooth paste. Cut the cauliflower into florets; cut the spring onions in half lengthways, then into short lengths; cut the snake beans into short lengths.
2 Heat half the oil in a wok, add the extra sliced garlic, stir-fry for 30 seconds or until just starting to brown; reserve some of garlic for a garnish.
3 Add the spinach to wok and stir-fry for another 30 seconds or until just wilted. Add pepper and remaining fish sauce and mix well. Arrange on a serving plate; keep warm.
4 Heat the remaining oil in the same wok; add the paste and cook over high heat for 1 minute or until fragrant. Add the cauliflower, stir-fry until well combined. Add water, bring to the boil; reduce heat, simmer covered for 3 minutes. Add beans; cover and cook for 3 minutes. Add spring onions and stir until just wilted. Spoon vegetables over the spinach; drizzle with lime juice and sprinkle with reserved fried garlic and spring onion tops.

Wash the snake beans, hold them in bunches and cut them into short lengths.

Add the extra sliced garlic to hot oil and stir-fry briefly until it starts to brown.

Stir in the remaining fish sauce and the pepper; toss to combine.

When the paste is well combined with the cauliflower, add the beans to the wok.

CUCUMBER SALAD WITH PEANUTS AND CHILLI

Preparation time: 25 minutes +
45 minutes marinating
Total cooking time: Nil
Serves 4–6

3 medium peeled cucumbers
2 tablespoons white vinegar

2 teaspoons white sugar
1–2 tablespoons Chilli Sauce
(see pages 100–101)
or commercial sauce
1/2 red onion, chopped
15 g (1/2 cup) fresh coriander
(cilantro) leaves
160 g (1 cup) roasted peanuts,
chopped
2 tablespoons crisp fried garlic
(see Glossary)

1/2 teaspoon chopped chilli
1 tablespoon fish sauce

1 Slice cucumbers in half lengthways. Remove seeds and slice thinly.
2 Stir vinegar and sugar in a large bowl until sugar dissolves. Toss with the cucumber, chilli sauce, onion and coriander. Marinate for 45 minutes.
3 Just before serving, add peanuts, garlic, chilli and fish sauce; toss lightly.

Use a teaspoon to remove the seeds from the peeled and halved cucumbers.

Toss vinegar and sugar mixture with the cucumber, sauce, onion and coriander.

Add the chopped peanuts, fried garlic, chillies and fish sauce and toss lightly.

VEGETABLE CURRY

Preparation time: 25 minutes
Total cooking time: 20 minutes
Serves 4–6

100 g (3½ oz) snake beans
1 tablespoon oil
1 medium onion, finely
    chopped
1–2 tablespoons Green Curry
    Paste (see page 102) or
    commercial paste
375 ml (1½ cups) coconut milk
250 ml (1 cup) water

1 medium red capsicum
    (pepper), cut into strips
150 g (5½ oz) broccoli, cut into
    florets
4 makrut (kaffir) lime leaves
2 medium zucchini (courgettes),
    sliced
150 g (2 cups) shredded cabbage
2 tablespoons fish sauce
2 tablespoons lime juice
2 teaspoons finely grated
    lime zest
2 teaspoons soft brown sugar

1 Cut snake beans into short lengths.
Heat the oil in a large wok or frying
pan. Add onions and curry paste to
wok; cook 3 minutes over medium heat,
stirring. Add coconut milk and water,
bring to the boil. Stir; reduce heat and
simmer, uncovered, for 5 minutes.
2 Add snake beans, capsicum, broccoli
and lime leaves to the wok. Cook,
uncovered, for 5 minutes. Add the
zucchini and cabbage to the wok, cook
for 3 minutes or until softened.
3 Add fish sauce, lime juice and zest,
and brown sugar; toss.

C O O K ' S   F I L E

Variation: Celery or green beans
could be substituted for snake beans.

*Wash the snake beans, hold them in
bunches and cut them into short lengths.*

*Add the sliced zucchini and the shredded
cabbage to the wok. Cook for 3 minutes.*

*Use two spoons to toss sauce, juice and
zest, and brown sugar through the curry.*

HOT AND TANGY PRAWN AND FRUIT SALAD

Preparation time: 20 minutes
Total cooking time: Nil
Serves 4–6

150 g (5½ oz) cooked prawns
    (shrimp)
½ green pawpaw
1 large green apple
1 firm green pear
½ pineapple

100 g (3½ oz) grapes
2 tablespoons crisp fried onion
    (see Glossary)
1 tablespoon crisp fried garlic
    (see Glossary)
7 g (¼ cup) coriander (cilantro)
    leaves

Dressing
60 ml (¼ cup) lime juice
2 teaspoons grated lime zest
1 tablespoon fish sauce
2 teaspoons soft brown sugar
    or palm sugar

1–2 teaspoons chopped red or
    green chillies

1 Peel the prawns; set aside. Peel the
pawpaw, remove seeds and cut flesh
into cubes. Chop the apple and pear.
2 Peel and core pineapple; chop flesh
into bite-sized pieces. Combine all fruit
with prawns in a chilled serving bowl.
3 To make Dressing: Combine
lime juice and zest, fish sauce, sugar
and chillies. Pour dressing over fruit
and prawns; toss well. Scatter onions,
garlic and coriander leaves on top.

*Peel the green pawpaw, using a sharp
knife, and then cut the flesh into cubes.*

*After peeling the pineapple, cut the flesh
into bite-sized pieces.*

*Place the dressing ingredients in a small
bowl and mix well.*

*Vegetable Curry (top) and Hot and Tangy
Prawn and Fruit Salad*

SPICY PORK SALAD
(Larb)

Preparation time: 20 minutes
Total cooking time: 8 minutes
Serves 4–6

2 stems lemon grass (white part only)
2 fresh green chillies
1 tablespoon oil
500 g (1 lb 2 oz) lean minced (ground) pork or beef
60 ml (¼ cup) lime juice
2 teaspoons finely grated lime zest
2–6 teaspoons Chilli Sauce (see pages 100–101) or commercial sauce
lettuce leaves, for serving
10 g (⅓ cup) coriander (cilantro) leaves
5 g (¼ cup) small mint leaves
1 small red onion, finely sliced
50 g (⅓ cup) roasted peanuts, chopped
25 g (¼ cup) crisp fried garlic (see Glossary)

1 Slice the lemon grass very finely and then finely chop the green chillies.
2 Heat oil in a wok or frying pan. Add lemon grass, chillies and minced pork to wok. Stir-fry the meat, breaking up any lumps as it cooks, over high heat for 6 minutes or until cooked through. Transfer to a bowl; allow to cool.
3 Add lime juice, zest, and the chilli sauce to cooled meat. Arrange lettuce leaves on a serving plate. Stir most of the coriander and mint leaves, onion, peanuts and fried garlic through the meat mixture. Distribute over lettuce and sprinkle the rest of the leaves, onion, peanuts and garlic over the top.

Slice the lemon grass very finely, using a sharp knife.

Use a wooden spoon or fork to break up any lumps of minced meat as it cooks.

When the meat has cooled, add the lime juice, zest and chilli sauce to the bowl.

VEGETABLES IN COCONUT MILK

Preparation time: 20 minutes
Total cooking time: 15 minutes
Serves 4

2 tablespoons oil
2 cloves garlic, finely
   chopped
5 cm (2 inch) piece of ginger,
   grated
2 teaspoons fresh green
   peppercorns, optional

1 medium eggplant (aubergine),
   diced
1 small sweet potato,
   diced
2 teaspoons water
100 g (3½ oz) green beans, cut
   into 5 cm (2 inch) pieces
½ bunch asparagus, cut into
   5 cm (2 inch) pieces
125 ml (½ cup) coconut milk
2 teaspoons fish sauce
approximately 12 English
   spinach leaves, trimmed
30 g (½ cup) Thai basil
   leaves

1 Heat the oil in a wok or heavy-based frying pan. Add the garlic, ginger and peppercorns, if using, to the wok and cook for 30 seconds. Add the eggplant, sweet potato and water to the wok; cook for 5 minutes over medium heat, stirring frequently.
2 Add the beans to the wok; cover and steam for 4 minutes, shaking the wok occasionally to prevent sticking.
3 Add asparagus and coconut milk to the wok; cook for 3 minutes or until the asparagus is just tender. Add fish sauce, spinach and basil; toss until spinach and basil soften slightly. Serve.

Add the diced eggplant, sweet potato and water to the wok. Cook for 5 minutes.

Cover the wok after adding the beans and steam the vegetables for 4 minutes.

Use 2 spoons to toss briefly until the spinach and basil have softened slightly.

CHICKEN, PRAWN AND GRAPEFRUIT SALAD

Preparation time: 20 minutes
Total cooking time: Nil
Serves 4–6

1 small pink or yellow
    grapefruit
6 medium cooked prawns
    (shrimp)
1/2 small green pawpaw or
    green mango (about 100 g or
    3 1/2 oz)
2 Roma (plum) tomatoes
1 orange, peeled and segmented
125 g (4 oz) cooked chicken,
    shredded or cut into bite-
    sized pieces
4 spring onions (scallions),
    sliced
2 cloves garlic, sliced
2 tablespoons coarsely chopped
    coriander (cilantro)
1 tablespoon desiccated
    coconut
lettuce leaves, for serving
1 tablespoon roasted, unsalted
    peanuts, finely chopped
2 teaspoons dried shrimp,
    finely chopped

Dressing
2 teaspoons soft brown sugar
1 1/2 tablespoons fish sauce
60 ml (1/4 cup) lime juice
2 teaspoons chilli sauce
    (see pages 100–101)
    or commercial sauce

1 Peel the grapefruit, discarding any white pith. Cut the fruit into thin segments. Peel the prawns, removing the tails; devein.
2 Peel the pawpaw and cut it into long, fine strips. Chop the tomatoes into bite-sized pieces.
3 Combine the pawpaw, grapefruit, prawns, tomatoes, orange segments, chicken, onions, garlic, coriander and coconut in a medium bowl.
4 To make Dressing: Combine the sugar, fish sauce, lime juice and chilli sauce in a small jug and whisk until the sugar has dissolved. Pour the dressing over the salad and toss gently. Serve the salad on a bed of lettuce leaves and sprinkle peanuts and dried shrimp over the top.

Peel the grapefruit, removing all the white pith. Cut into thin segments.

Cut the peeled pawpaw into long, fine strips, using a sharp knife.

Combine the fruit, chicken, onions, garlic, coriander and coconut in a bowl.

Whisk the dressing ingredients until the sugar has dissolved.

CRISP ONION WITH CABBAGE SALAD

Preparation time: 20 minutes
Total cooking time: Nil
Serves 4–6

1/2 red capsicum (pepper)
1/2 medium Chinese or
    curly white cabbage
35 g (1/2 cup) crisp fried onion
    (see Glossary)

25 g (1/4 cup) crisp fried garlic
    (see Glossary)
15 g (1/4 cup) mint leaves,
    shredded
80 ml (1/3 cup) coconut milk
1 tablespoon fish sauce
1 teaspoon soft brown sugar
2 fresh red chillies, finely sliced
lime wedges

1 Cut the capsicum into fine strips.
2 Finely shred cabbage using a large knife or cleaver. Arrange shredded cabbage on a serving platter, then sprinkle onions, garlic, capsicum and mint over the top. Place the coconut milk, fish sauce and brown sugar in a jug and stir until well combined.
3 Pour the dressing over the salad. Sprinkle with chillies and serve with lime wedges on the side.

COOK'S FILE

Storage time: Pour the dressing over vegetables just before serving, to prevent salad becoming soggy.

Using a long-bladed, sharp knife, cut half a red capsicum into very fine strips.

Cut the cabbage into fine shreds, using a sharp knife or cleaver.

Mix the coconut milk, fish sauce and sugar in a jug and pour over the salad.

CRISP FISH WITH SALAD

Preparation time: 20 minutes
Total cooking time: 15 minutes
Serves 4

400 g (14 oz) white fish fillets
40 g (¹/3 cup) cornflour
   (cornstarch)
60 ml (¹/4 cup) oil
1 large green mango (about 400 g
   or 14 oz)
1 small red onion, halved and
   thinly sliced
2 tablespoons coarsely chopped
   mint leaves

2 tablespoons coarsely chopped
   coriander (cilantro)
lettuce leaves, for serving
1 tablespoon roasted unsalted
   peanuts

Dressing
2 small green chillies, chopped
2 tablespoons fish sauce
60 ml (¹/4 cup) lime juice
2 teaspoons soft brown sugar

1 Poach or steam the fish fillets until cooked; remove from pan and cool. Process in a food processor until finely chopped, but not puréed. Transfer to a bowl and mix in cornflour. If mixture

is too wet, add a little more cornflour.
2 Mould tablespoonsful of the mixture into thin, irregular patties. Heat the oil in a frying pan and cook patties a few at a time until well browned and crisp. Drain on paper towels.
3 Peel the mango and cut the flesh into thin shreds. Combine the mango, onion, chopped mint and coriander, in a medium bowl. Arrange on a serving plate, on a bed of lettuce leaves. Fish patties can be broken into halves or quarters before serving with the salad.
4 To make Dressing: Place all the ingredients in a bowl and blend until smooth. Pour the dressing over the salad and sprinkle with peanuts.

Steam or poach the fish fillets. They are cooked when they flake easily with a fork.

Using your hands, mould tablespoons of the mixture into thin, irregular patties.

Peel the green mango and cut the flesh into long, thin shreds.

WATERCRESS AND DUCK SALAD WITH LYCHEES

Preparation time: 25 minutes
Total cooking time: 30 minutes
Serves 4

2 large duck breasts, with the
   skin on
1 tablespoon soy sauce
1/2 each of 1 red, green and
   yellow capsicum (pepper)
1/2 bunch watercress
12 fresh lychees, or 1 large can
2 tablespoons pickled
   shredded ginger

1–2 tablespoons green
   peppercorns, optional
1 tablespoon white vinegar
2 teaspoons soft brown sugar
1–2 teaspoons chopped fresh
   red chillies
15 g (1/2 cup) coriander
   (cilantro) leaves

1 Preheat the oven to hot 210°C (415°F/Gas 6–7). Brush the duck fillets with the soy sauce and place on a rack inside a baking tray. Bake for 30 minutes. Remove from the oven and allow to cool.
2 Remove the membrane and seeds from the capsicums and slice the flesh into thin strips. Pick the leaves from the watercress. Peel the fresh lychees and remove the seeds or, if using canned lychees, drain them.
3 Arrange the watercress, capsicum strips, ginger and lychees on a large serving platter. Slice the duck into thin pieces and arrange over the salad. In a small bowl, combine the peppercorns, if using, vinegar, sugar, chillies and coriander leaves. Serve on the side, for spooning over the salad.

COOK'S FILE

Note: Pickled ginger is available from Asian food speciality stores.

Brush the duck all over with soy sauce.

Peel the fresh lychees and remove the seeds from each.

Using a sharp knife, slice the duck into thin pieces.

BEEF WITH CUCUMBER AND TOMATO

Preparation time: 20 minutes
Total cooking time: 5 minutes
Serves 4

1 tablespoon oil
2 cloves garlic, chopped
2 teaspoons chopped fresh
    red chillies
1 teaspoon black pepper
3 fresh coriander (cilantro)
    roots, finely chopped
2 teaspoons oil, extra
350 g (12 oz) rib eye or sirloin
    steak
2 medium tomatoes or
    12 cherry tomatoes
1 medium cucumber
2 tablespoons fish sauce
Tamarind and Chilli Dipping
    Sauce (see page 101)

1 Combine the oil, garlic, chillies, pepper and coriander in a mortar and pestle or small-bowled food processor. Pound or process until mixture forms a paste. Spread paste over the steak.
2 Oil a cast iron frying pan or grill plate and heat until very hot; cook the steak 2 minutes each side, turning once only. Wrap in foil, cool completely.
3 Chop the tomatoes or halve the cherry tomatoes. Cut cucumber into thick chunks. Combine the tomato, cucumber and fish sauce; toss. Slice steak into thin strips, arrange on plates and accompany with the tomato and cucumber salad, and sauce.

COOK'S FILE

Note: Cook steak until medium rare; do not overcook. Allow it to stand for at least 5 minutes before slicing.

Use a knife to spread the paste evenly over the steak.

On cast iron pan or grill plate, cook steak for 2 minutes each side, turning once.

If using cherry tomatoes, cut them all in half with a sharp knife.

SPICY STEAMED CORN

Preparation time: 25 minutes
Total cooking time: 20–25 minutes
Serves 4

4 corn cobs or 16 baby
corn spears
5 cm (2 inch) piece fresh ginger,
    grated
1–3 teaspoons chopped fresh
    red chillies

3 cloves garlic, chopped
2 teaspoons green peppercorns,
    crushed
2 tablespoons water
2 tablespoons fish sauce

1 Remove the husks and all the silk from the cobs. If using corn cobs, cut them into smaller pieces. In a medium bowl, place ginger, chillies, garlic, peppercorns and water; mix together well.
2 Press the spice mixture onto the corn cobs and place in a steaming basket lined with banana leaves or baking paper.
3 Place the basket over a wok or pan of boiling water; cover and steam for 20 minutes, or until the corn is tender. Sprinkle the corn with the fish sauce and serve immediately.

COOK'S FILE

Notes: Bamboo steaming baskets are inexpensive to buy. Always line the base to prevent the food falling through the cracks.

Remove the husks and all the silk from the corn cobs.

Use your fingers to press the prepared spice mixture onto the corn cobs.

Line a steamer basket with banana leaves or baking paper. Place cobs on lining.

RED VEGETABLE CURRY

Preparation time: 25 minutes
Total cooking time: 25–30 minutes
Serves 4

1 tablespoon oil
1 medium onion, chopped
1–2 tablespoons Red Curry
   Paste (see page 102) or
   commercial paste
375 ml (1½ cups) coconut milk
250 ml (1 cup) water
2 medium potatoes (350 g or
   12 oz), chopped
200 g (7 oz) cauliflower florets

6 makrut (kaffir) lime leaves
150 g (5½ oz) snake beans, cut
   into 3 cm (1¼ inch) pieces
½ red capsicum (pepper), cut
   into strips
10 fresh baby corn spears, cut
   in half lengthways
1 tablespoon green peppercorns,
   roughly chopped
15 g (¼ cup) Thai basil leaves,
   finely chopped
2 tablespoons fish sauce
1 tablespoon lime juice
2 teaspoons soft brown sugar

1 Heat the oil in a large wok or frying pan. Cook onion and curry paste for 4 minutes over medium heat, stirring constantly.
2 Add the coconut milk and water, bring to the boil and simmer, uncovered, for 5 minutes. Add the potatoes, cauliflower and makrut lime leaves and simmer for 7 minutes. Add the snake beans, capsicum, corn and peppercorns, cook for 5 minutes or until the vegetables are tender.
3 Add the basil, fish sauce, lime juice and sugar. Serve with steamed rice.

COOK'S FILE

Hints: If fresh baby corn spears are not available, use canned baby corn—add just before serving.

Stir the chopped onion and curry paste in a wok for 4 minutes over medium heat.

Add the snake beans, capsicum, corn and peppercorns, and cook until tender.

When vegetables are tender, add the basil, fish sauce, lime juice and sugar.

Peel the sweet potato and cut it into even-sized cubes.

When simmering the coconut milk, don't cover the pan or the milk will curdle.

Add the eggplant and makrut lime leaves to wok; cook until vegetables are tender.

Use 2 wooden spoons to toss vegetables with the sauce, juice, zest and sugar.

GREEN VEGETABLE CURRY WITH SWEET POTATO AND EGGPLANT

Preparation time: 25 minutes
Total cooking time: 30 minutes
Serves 4–6

1 tablespoon oil
1 medium onion, chopped
1–2 tablespoons Green Curry
　　Paste (page 102) or
　　commercial paste
1 medium sweet potato
375 ml (1½ cups) coconut milk
250 ml (1 cup) water
1 medium eggplant (aubergine)
　　(200 g or 7 oz), sliced
6 makrut (kaffir) lime leaves
2 tablespoons fish sauce
2 tablespoons lime juice
2 teaspoons lime zest
2 teaspoons soft brown sugar
1 sprig coriander (cilantro)

1 Heat the oil in a large wok or frying pan. Add the onion and curry paste to the wok and stir for 3 minutes over medium heat. Cut the sweet potato into cubes.
2 Add the coconut milk and water to the wok. Bring to the boil; reduce heat and simmer, uncovered, for 5 minutes. Add the sweet potato to the wok; cook for 6 minutes.
3 Add the eggplant and lime leaves to the wok; cook for 10 minutes, or until the vegetables are very tender, stirring occasionally.
4 Add the fish sauce, lime juice and zest, and sugar; toss. Sprinkle with some fresh coriander leaves. You can garnish the curry with extra lime leaves if you like. Serve with steamed rice.

COOK'S FILE

Notes: Traditional Thai, pea-sized eggplants (aubergines) can be used, instead of the sliced eggplant. Add them to the curry about six minutes before serving. They are available, when in season, from Asian fruit and vegetable stores.

PRAWN SALAD WITH COCONUT MILK DRESSING

Preparation time: 30 minutes
Total cooking time: 10 minutes
Serves 4

12 large raw prawns (shrimp)
2 tablespoons lime juice
2 teaspoons finely grated
　　lime zest
3 teaspoons soft brown sugar
1 medium orange
1 red capsicum (pepper)
1 yellow capsicum (pepper)
125 ml (1/2 cup) coconut cream

2 tablespoons fish sauce
7 g (1/4 cup) fresh coriander
　　(cilantro) leaves
3 makrut (kaffir) lime leaves,
　　finely shredded

1 Peel the raw prawns, leaving the tails intact. Cut down the back of the prawns; devein. Simmer the prawns in a pot of salted water until they turn bright pink. Remove prawns from the water, using a slotted spoon and place them in a bowl of cold water; allow to cool. Drain and then combine in a bowl with the lime juice, zest and brown sugar. Set aside for 15 minutes.
2 Peel the orange, trimming away all the white pith, and separate into

segments. Seed both capsicums into thin strips. Arrange orange segments and capsicum strips on a serving plate. Place prawns in centre of salad.
3 In a bowl, whisk together the coconut cream and fish sauce; drizzle over the salad. Garnish with the coriander and shredded lime leaves. Serve immediately.

COOK'S FILE

Variation: Cooked large prawns can be used. Leave them in their shells and arrange on the salad.
• Remove all the white pith from the orange as it has a bitter taste. Pull off the membrane from each segment to make the orange easier to eat.

Transfer the cooked prawns to a bowl of cold water and allow them to cool.

Use a sharp knife to peel the orange, removing all the white pith.

Just before serving, whisk the coconut cream and fish sauce in a bowl.

STIR-FRIED MUSHROOMS

Preparation time: 10 minutes
Total cooking time: 6 minutes
Serves 4

2 cloves garlic
3 cm (1 1/4 inch) piece galangal
2 red chillies
1 tablespoon oil
200 g (7 oz) button mushrooms,
　　halved

100 g (3 1/2 oz) oyster
　　mushrooms, halved
1 tablespoon fish sauce
1 teaspoon soy sauce
30 g (1/2 cup) chopped Thai basil

1 Chop the garlic. Finely slice the galangal and chillies. Heat the oil in a wok or frying pan.
2 Add the galangal, garlic and chillies to the wok and stir for 2 minutes. Add the button mushrooms and stir-fry for 2 minutes. Add the oyster

mushrooms; cook for approximately 30 seconds, tossing constantly until the mushrooms begin to soften.
3 Add the fish sauce, soy sauce and chopped basil, toss well. Serve as a side dish to accompany main courses and steamed rice.

COOK'S FILE

Variation: Fresh shiitake, Swiss brown, straw, or any other variety of fresh mushrooms, according to availability, may be used.

Finely slice the piece of galangal, using a sharp knife.

Cook the oyster mushrooms briefly, until they begin to soften.

Toss in the fish sauce, soy sauce and chopped basil.

Prawn Salad with Coconut Milk Dressing
(top) and Stir-fried Mushrooms

GOLDEN FRIED EGGPLANT AND CABBAGE

Preparation time: 20 minutes
Total cooking time: 6–7 minutes
Serves 4

2 medium eggplants
    (aubergines)
2 tablespoons oil
3 spring onions (scallions),
    chopped
3 cloves garlic, chopped

1 tablespoon soft brown sugar
2 teaspoons soy sauce
1/4 Chinese or curly white
    cabbage, shredded
2 tablespoons lime juice
2 teaspoons fish sauce
1 chilli, finely sliced

1 Slice the eggplants and cut the slices into small wedges. Heat the oil in a wok or large frying pan. Add the onions and garlic and then stir for 1 minute, over medium heat.

2 Add the sugar and eggplant to the wok, and stir-fry for 3 minutes or until eggplant is golden brown. Add soy sauce, cabbage and lime juice to wok.

3 Toss well and then cover and steam for 30 seconds or until cabbage softens slightly. Add the fish sauce, toss and serve immediately, sprinkled with the sliced chilli.

COOK'S FILE

Note: Thai eggplants can be purple or striped purple and white. They range from tiny pea-sized to golf ball sized, to small zucchini sized eggplants. Any type may be used. Alter cooking time accordingly.

Slice 2 medium eggplants and cut the slices into small wedges.

Add the sugar and eggplant to the wok and stir-fry until golden brown.

Cover the wok and steam until the cabbage has softened.

PEPPERED STIR-FRIED ASPARAGUS

Preparation time: 20 minutes
Total cooking time: 4–5 minutes
Serves 4

1 tablespoon green peppercorns
15 g (¹/2 cup) coriander
    (cilantro) leaves and stems
1 tablespoon oil
220 g (¹/2 bunch) snake beans,
    cut into short lengths

150 g (1 bunch) asparagus, cut
    into short lengths
2 cloves garlic, chopped
1 teaspoon soft brown sugar
2 teaspoons water
1 tablespoon fish sauce
1 teaspoon chopped red or
    green chillies

1 Finely crush the peppercorns and chop the coriander leaves and stems. Place in a bowl and mix well.
2 Heat the oil in a wok or frying pan. Add pepper and coriander mixture, snake beans, asparagus, garlic and sugar to the wok; stir-fry for 30 seconds over medium heat.
3 Add the water to wok, cover and steam for 2 minutes or until vegetables are just tender. Season with fish sauce. Stir through the chilli and garnish with extra chilli, if desired.

C O O K ' S   F I L E

Variation: If snake beans are not readily available, you can substitute with normal green beans or peeled broad beans.

Finely crush the peppercorns, using the flat side of a knife or a cleaver.

Add pepper and coriander mixture, garlic, snake beans, asparagus and sugar to wok.

Toss through the chopped chilli and stir in, just before serving.

Sauces

There is a variety of chilli sauces—choose whichever you prefer for use in recipes and as accompaniments.

COOKED HOT CHILLI SAUCE

Chop 2 cloves of garlic and combine in a dry frying pan with 2 stems of finely chopped lemon grass, 6 chopped French shallots (eschallots), 2–4 tablespoons of chopped red chillies and 2 chopped coriander (cilantro) roots. Stir for 5 minutes over low heat; allow to cool. Place in a food processor with 2 teaspoons of shrimp paste and 2 tablespoons of soft brown sugar. Process for 20 seconds at a time, scraping down the sides of the bowl, until the mixture forms a smooth paste. Add 2 tablespoons of fish sauce and 60 ml ($^1/4$ cup) of cold water; process until smooth. For a thinner consistency add 60–125 ml ($^1/4$–$^1/2$ cup) of water. Refrigerate in an airtight container for up to 1 month.

QUICK CHILLI SAUCE

Trim stems from 6 large, red chillies; cut chillies open (remove seeds for milder flavour). Soak for 15 minutes in hot water. Process in a food processor with 1 tablespoon of chopped red chillies, 60 ml ($^1/4$ cup) of white vinegar, 80 g ($^1/3$ cup) of caster (superfine) sugar, 1 teaspoon of salt and 4 cloves of chopped garlic, until smooth. Cook in a pan for 15 minutes over medium heat, stirring frequently until thickened. Allow to cool; stir in 2 teaspoons of fish sauce.
Note: For Sweet Chilli Sauce, use 230 g (1 cup) sugar.

BASIC DIPPING SAUCE (NAM PRIK)

Combine 60 ml ($^1/4$ cup) of fish sauce, 1 tablespoon of white vinegar, 2–3 teaspoons of finely chopped red chillies, 1 teaspoon of sugar and 2 teaspoons of chopped coriander (cilantro) stems; stir until sugar dissolves.

SOUR DIPPING SAUCE

In a bowl, combine 60 ml ($^{1}/4$ cup) of fish sauce, 2 tablespoons of white vinegar and 2 tablespoons of lime juice. Chopped coriander (cilantro) leaves may be added.

TAMARIND AND CHILLI DIPPING SAUCE

Heat 1 tablespoon of oil in a wok; add 4 finely chopped French shallots (eschallots) and 2 cloves of chopped garlic; stir for 2 minutes over low heat. Add 1–2 teaspoons of chopped fresh red chillies; cook for 30 seconds. Add 80 g ($^{1}/4$ cup) of tamarind purée and 1 tablespoon of soft brown sugar. Bring to the boil, stirring, simmer for 5 minutes. Allow to cool before serving; season with lime juice.

Clockwise, from top right:
Green Mango Hot Sauce; Tamarind and
Chilli Dipping Sauce; Sour Dipping Sauce;
Basic Dipping Sauce (Nam Prik); Quick
Chilli Sauce; Cooked Hot Chilli Sauce

GREEN MANGO HOT SAUCE

Combine 2 cloves of chopped garlic, 3 chopped French shallots (eschallots), $^{1}/4$ teaspoon of freshly ground black pepper, 1 teaspoon of dried shrimp and 1 teaspoon of shrimp paste in a mortar and pestle or small-bowled food processor. Pound or process until fine; stir in 1 tablespoon of soft brown sugar, $^{1}/2$ finely grated green mango and 2 tablespoons of cold water. Use within 12 hours.

101

Pastes

RED CURRY PASTE

1 tablespoon coriander seeds
2 teaspoons cumin seeds
1 teaspoon black peppercorns
2 teaspoons dried shrimp paste
1 teaspoon ground nutmeg
12 dried or fresh red chillies, roughly chopped
155 g (1 cup) French shallots (eschallots),
    chopped
2 tablespoons oil
4 stems lemon grass (white part only),
    finely chopped
12 small cloves garlic, chopped
2 tablespoons coriander (cilantro) roots, chopped
2 tablespoons coriander (cilantro) stems, chopped
6 makrut (kaffir) lime leaves, chopped
2 teaspoons grated lime zest
2 teaspoons salt
2 teaspoons turmeric
1 teaspoon paprika

1 Place the coriander and cumin seeds in a dry frying pan and heat for 2–3 minutes, shaking the pan constantly.
2 Place the roasted spices and peppercorns in a mortar and pestle or clean coffee grinder and work them until they are finely ground. Wrap the shrimp paste in a small amount of foil and cook under a hot grill for 3 minutes, turning the package twice.
3 Process the ground spices, roasted shrimp paste, nutmeg and chillies in a food processor for 5 seconds. Add the remaining ingredients and process for 20 seconds at a time, scraping down the sides of the bowl with a spatula each time, until the mixture forms a smooth paste.
Makes approximately 1 cup

GREEN CURRY PASTE

1 tablespoon coriander seeds
2 teaspoons cumin seeds
1 teaspoon black peppercorns
2 teaspoons dried shrimp paste
8 large fresh green chillies, roughly chopped
155 g (1 cup) French shallots (eschallots),
    chopped
5 cm (2 inch) galangal, pounded or chopped
12 small cloves garlic, chopped
30 g (1 cup) chopped coriander (cilantro) leaves,
    stems and roots
6 makrut (kaffir) lime leaves, chopped
3 stems lemon grass (white part only),
    finely chopped
2 teaspoons grated lime zest
2 teaspoons salt
2 tablespoons oil

1 Place the coriander and cumin seeds in a dry frying pan and heat for 2–3 minutes, shaking the pan constantly.
2 Place the roasted spices and peppercorns in a mortar and pestle or clean coffee grinder and work them until they are finely ground. Wrap the shrimp paste in a small amount of foil and cook under a hot grill for 2–3 minutes, turning the package twice.
3 Process the ground spices and shrimp paste in a food processor for 5 seconds. Add the remaining ingredients and process for 20 seconds at a time, scraping down the sides of the bowl with a spatula each time, until the mixture forms a smooth paste.
Makes approximately 1 cup

PANANG CURRY PASTE

8 large dried red chillies
125 ml (1/2 cup) hot water
2 teaspoons shrimp paste
80 g (1/2 cup) French shallots (eschallots), chopped
5 cm (2 inch) fresh galangal, pounded or chopped
12 small cloves garlic, chopped
4 coriander (cilantro) roots, chopped
3 stems lemon grass (white part only),
    finely chopped
1 tablespoon grated lime zest
1 teaspoon black peppercorns
2 tablespoons oil
1 tablespoon fish sauce
1 teaspoon salt
125 g (1/2 cup) crunchy peanut butter

1 Trim the stems from the chillies and soak them in hot water for 30 minutes.
2 Wrap the shrimp paste in a small amount of foil and cook under a hot grill for 2–3 minutes, turning the package twice. Place the softened chillies and soaking water, shrimp paste, shallots, galangal, garlic, coriander root, lemon grass, lime zest, peppercorns and oil in a food processor. Process for 20 seconds at a time, scraping down the sides of the bowl with a spatula each time, until the mixture forms a smooth paste.
3 Add the fish sauce, salt and peanut butter; process for 10 seconds or until combined.
Makes approximately 1 cup

MUSAMAN CURRY PASTE

1 tablespoon coriander seeds
1 tablespoon cumin seeds
seeds from 4 cardamom pods
2 teaspoons black peppercorns
1 tablespoon shrimp paste
1 teaspoon nutmeg
1/2 teaspoon ground cloves
15 dried red chillies
80 g (1/2 cup) chopped French shallots (eschallots)
2 stems lemon grass (white part only),
    finely chopped
6 small cloves garlic, chopped
1 tablespoon oil

1 Place the coriander, cumin and cardamom seeds in a dry frying pan and heat for 2–3 minutes, shaking the pan constantly.
2 Place the spices and peppercorns in a mortar and pestle or a clean coffee grinder and work or grind until they are finely ground.
3 Place the ground spices and remaining ingredients in a food processor. Process for 20 seconds and scrape down the sides of the bowl with a spatula. Process for 5 seconds at a time until the mixture forms a smooth paste.
Makes approximately 1 cup

STORAGE FOR ALL CURRY PASTES

Fresh paste will keep for up to 3 weeks in an airtight container in the refrigerator. Alternatively, place table-spoonsful in an ice-cube tray, cover and freeze for several hours; release cubes into a freezer bag. Place the bag in the freezer and use the cubes when required. Allow to defrost for 30 minutes at room temperature before using. Frozen paste will keep for up to 4 months.

DELICIOUS DESSERTS

FRUIT PLATTER

Preparation time: 25 minutes +
  cooling time
Total cooking time: 15 minutes
Serves 4–6

460 g (2 cups) caster
  (superfine) sugar
500 ml (2 cups) water
2 tablespoons lemon or lime juice
5 cm (2 inch) strip lemon or
  lime zest
1 small pineapple, chopped
1 pawpaw, shaped into balls
  or chopped
1 rockmelon, shaped into
  balls or chopped
1 honeydew melon, shaped
  into balls or chopped
8 fresh lychees, peeled
  and seeded
mint leaves or sprigs,
  to garnish

1 Place the sugar and water in a medium pan. Stir over medium heat, without boiling, for 5 minutes or until the sugar is dissolved. Add the juice and zest to the pan and then bring to the boil. Boil, without stirring, for 10 minutes or until the syrup has thickened slightly.

2 Remove the zest from the pan and set the mixture aside to cool. Place the prepared fruit in a large bowl; cover and chill for at least 30 minutes. Just prior to serving, pour over enough cooled syrup to coat the fruit and then carefully fold it through. Arrange the fruit in an attractive bowl, platter or hollowed out melon. Garnish with mint leaves or sprigs.

COOK'S FILE

Storage time: The syrup can be prepared a day ahead and refrigerated. However, the fruit is best prepared on the day of serving.
Hint: Quarters or halves of limes are attractive served on the side.
Variation: Add any tropical fruits that are in season, such as Fijian or Hawaiian pawpaw, rambutan, starfruit and mangosteens.

Peel lychees and squeeze out the seeds by pressing with your thumb and forefinger.

Using a fork or slotted spoon, remove the zest from the syrup and discard.

COCONUT ICE CREAM
(I-Tim Kati)

Preparation time: 10 minutes +
   freezing
Total cooking time: 15 minutes
Makes about 900 ml (4 cups)

425 g (15 oz) can coconut cream
375 ml (1½ cups) cream
2 eggs
2 egg yolks
115 g (½ cup) caster (superfine)
   sugar
¼ teaspoon salt
1 teaspoon vanilla essence
fresh mint leaves and toasted,
   shredded coconut, to garnish

1 Place the coconut cream and cream in a medium pan. Stir over medium heat, without boiling, for 2–3 minutes. Set aside; cover and keep warm. Place the eggs, egg yolks, sugar, salt and vanilla in a large heatproof bowl. With electric beaters, beat the mixture for 2–3 minutes until frothy and thickened. Place bowl over a pan of simmering water.
2 Continue to beat the egg mixture while gradually adding the warm coconut mixture, 60 ml (¼ cup) at a time, until all the coconut mixture is added. This process will take about 10 minutes—continue until the custard thickens. The mixture will be the consistency of thin cream and should easily coat the back of a spoon. Do not allow to boil or it will curdle.
3 Cover and set aside to cool. Stir the mixture occasionally while cooling. When cool, pour into a 20 x 30 cm (8 x 12 inch) baking tin, cover and freeze for 1½ hours or until half-frozen.
4 Quickly spoon the mixture into a food processor and process for 30 seconds, or until smooth. Return to the baking tin or place in plastic containers; cover and freeze completely. Coconut ice cream looks attractive if served in scoops and garnished with mint and coconut.

COOK'S FILE

Storage time: Store for up to three weeks in the freezer.

Beat the mixture until it is thick and frothy, using electric beaters.

Cook the coconut mixture until it easily coats the back of a spoon.

Pour the cooled mixture into a baking tin; cover and freeze until half-frozen.

Transfer the half-frozen mixture into a food processor and process until smooth.

Place the cinnamon sticks, nutmeg, cloves, cream and water in a pan.

Stir in the sugar and coconut milk and return the pan to the heat.

Strain the custard into a jug and discard the whole spices.

Insert a knife in the centre of one of the custards to check if they are set.

SPICY COCONUT CUSTARD

Preparation time: 20 minutes
Total cooking time: 55–60 minutes
Serves 8

2 cinnamon sticks
1 teaspoon ground nutmeg
2 teaspoons whole cloves
300 ml (10½ fl oz) cream
250 ml (1 cup) water
90 g (½ cup) chopped palm sugar
280 g (10 oz) can coconut milk
3 eggs, lightly beaten
2 egg yolks, lightly beaten

1 Preheat the oven to warm 160°C (315°F/Gas 2–3). Place spices, cream and water in a medium pan. Bring to simmering point; reduce the heat to very low and leave for 5 minutes to allow the spices to flavour the liquid.

2 Add the sugar and coconut milk to the pan; return to low heat and stir until the sugar has dissolved.

3 Whisk the eggs and egg yolks in a medium bowl until combined. Pour the spiced mixture over the eggs; stir to combine. Strain into a jug; discard the whole spices. Pour the custard mixture into eight 125 ml (½-cup) dishes. Place in a baking dish; pour in hot water to come halfway up the sides. Bake for 40–45 minutes.

4 Insert a knife in the centre of one of the custards to check if they are set; the mixture should be only slightly wobbly. Remove custards from the baking dish. Serve hot or chilled, with whipped cream and toasted coconut shreds for a special occasion.

COOK'S FILE

Storage time: The custards will keep, covered and refrigerated, for up to three days.

BANANAS IN LIME JUICE WITH COCONUT PANCAKES

Preparation time: 10 minutes
Total cooking time: 30 minutes
Serves 4–6

40 g (1/3 cup) plain (all-purpose) flour
2 tablespoons rice flour
55 g (1/4 cup) caster (superfine) sugar
25 g (1/4 cup) desiccated coconut
250 ml (1 cup) coconut milk
1 egg, lightly beaten
butter
4 large bananas
60 g (1/4 cup) butter
60 g (1/3 cup) soft brown sugar
80 ml (1/3 cup) lime juice
1 tablespoon shredded, toasted coconut, for serving
strips of lime zest, for serving

1 Sift the flours into a medium bowl. Add sugar and coconut and mix through with a spoon. Make a well in the centre, pour in the combined coconut milk and egg, and then beat until smooth.

2 Heat a non-stick frying pan or crepe pan and melt a little butter in it. Pour 60 ml (1/4 cup) of the pancake mixture in the pan. Cook it over medium heat until the underside is golden.

3 Turn the pancake over and cook the other side. Transfer to a plate and cover with a tea towel to keep warm. Repeat the process with the remaining pancake batter, greasing the pan when necessary. Keep the pancakes warm while preparing the bananas.

4 Cut the bananas diagonally into thick slices. Heat the butter in the pan; add bananas and toss until coated. Cook over medium heat until bananas start to soften and brown. Sprinkle with the brown sugar and stir gently until it has melted. Stir in lime juice. Serve as a stack, layering bananas and some sauce between each pancake. Sprinkle with extra coconut and lime zest; cut into wedges and serve.

COOK'S FILE

Hint: These pancakes can be turned over more easily if slid onto a plate and then inverted back into the pan.

Pour combined coconut milk and egg into the centre and beat with a wooden spoon.

Pour 60 ml (1/4 cup) of the pancake mixture into a heated, greased pan.

Using a spatula, turn the pancake over to cook the other side.

Add the lime juice to the bananas just before serving.

MANGO ICE CREAM

Preparation time: 10 minutes +
  freezing
Total cooking time: Nil
Makes about 900 ml (4 cups)

400 g (1 packet) frozen mango
115 g (¹/2 cup) caster
  (superfine) sugar
60 ml (¹/4 cup) mango or apricot
  nectar
300 ml (10¹/2 fl oz) cream

mango slices and mint sprigs to
  garnish

1 Defrost the mango until it is soft enough to mash but still icy. Place the mango in a medium bowl and add the sugar and nectar. Stir for 1–2 minutes or until the sugar has dissolved.

2 Beat the cream in a small bowl until stiff peaks form. Gently fold the cream through the mango mixture.

3 Spoon the mixture into a baking tray; cover and freeze for about 1¹/2 hours or until half-frozen. Quickly spoon the mixture into a food processor. Process for 30 seconds or until smooth. Return to the tray or plastic container; cover and freeze completely (for at least 8 hours). Remove the ice cream from the freezer for 15 minutes before serving, to allow it to soften a little. Serve the ice cream in scoops with mango slices and sprigs of mint.

COOK'S FILE

Storage time: Up to 3 weeks.
Variation: When available, use fresh mangoes instead of frozen mangoes.

Add the sugar and nectar to the defrosted mango and stir until sugar dissolves.

Using electric beaters, beat the cream until stiff peaks form.

Quickly spoon the half-frozen mixture into the food processor.

STICKY RICE WITH MANGOES
(Kaow Niaw Mamuang)

Preparation time: 40 minutes
+ 12 hours standing time
Total cooking time: 60–65 minutes
Serves 4

400 g (2 cups) glutinous rice
250 ml (1 cup) coconut milk
90 g (1/2 cup) chopped palm
  sugar
1/4 teaspoon salt
2–3 mangoes, peeled, seeded
  and sliced
3 tablespoons coconut cream
1 tablespoon sesame
  seeds, toasted
fresh mint sprigs, to garnish

1 Place the rice in a sieve and wash under running water until the water runs clear. Place in a glass or ceramic bowl; cover with water and leave to soak overnight, or for a minimum of 12 hours. Drain the rice.
2 Line a metal or bamboo steamer with muslin. Place the rice on top of the muslin; cover with tight-fitting lid. Place the steamer over a pot of boiling water. Steam over medium-low heat for 50 minutes, or until rice is cooked. Remove from heat; transfer to a large bowl and fluff up the rice with a fork.
3 Pour the coconut milk into a small pan; add the palm sugar and salt. Bring slowly to the boil, stirring constantly until the sugar has dissolved. Lower the heat; simmer for 5 minutes until the mixture is slightly thickened. Stir often while it is simmering, and take care that the mixture does not stick on the bottom of the pan.
4 Pour the coconut milk slowly over the top of the rice. Use a fork to lift and fluff the rice. Do not stir liquid through, otherwise rice will become too gluggy. Allow rice mixture to rest for 20 minutes before carefully spooning it into the centre of 4 warmed serving plates. Arrange mango slices around the mounds. Spoon a little coconut cream over rice and sprinkle with sesame seeds. Garnish with mint leaves.

Wash glutinous rice in a strainer under cold water until water runs clear.

Line a steamer with muslin and place the drained rice on top of the muslin.

Stir the coconut milk, palm sugar and salt until slightly thickened.

Pour the coconut milk mixture slowly over the top of the cooked rice.

INDEX

USEFUL INFORMATION

All our recipes are tested in our test kitchen. Standard metric measuring cups and spoons are used in the development of our recipes. All cup and spoon measurements are level. We have used 60 g (2¼ oz/ Grade 3) eggs in all recipes. Sizes of cans vary from manufacturer to manufacturer and between countries—use the can size closest to the one in the recipe.

Conversion Guide

1 cup	= 250 ml (9 fl oz)
1 teaspoon	= 5 ml
1 Australian tablespoon	= 20 ml (4 teaspoons)
1 UK/US tablespoon	≐ 15 ml (3 teaspoons)

Note: We have used 20 ml tablespoon measures. If you are using a 15 ml tablespoon, for most recipes the difference will not be noticeable. However, for recipes using baking powder, gelatine, bicarbonate of soda, small amounts of flour and cornflour, add an extra teaspoon for each tablespoon specified.

Cup Conversions

1 cup basil leaves, whole	= 50 g (1¾ oz)
chopped	= 60 g (2¼ oz)
1 cup bean sprouts	= 90 g (3¼ oz)
1 cup cabbage, finely shredded	= 50 g (1¾ oz)
1 cup cornflour	= 125 g (4½ oz)
1 cup flour, plain or self-raising	= 125 g (4½ oz)
1 cup peanuts	= 175 g (6 oz)
1 cup peas, green	= 160 g (5½ oz)
1 cup rice flour	= 175 g (6 oz)
1 cup rice, short-grain, raw	= 185 g (6 oz)
long-grain, raw	= 185 g (6 oz)
1 cup sugar, demerara	= 220 g (8 oz)
soft brown	= 185 g (6 oz)

Oven Temperatures

Cooking times may vary slightly depending on the individual oven. We suggest you check the manufacturer's instructions to ensure proper temperature control. **For fan-forced ovens** check your appliance manual, but as a general rule, set oven temperature to 20°C lower than the temperature indicated in the recipe.

International Glossary

broad bean	fava bean
capsicum	pepper
chilli	chili pepper, chile
coriander	cilantro
cos lettuce	romaine
cream	single/pouring cream
cream, thick	double/heavy cream
fish sauce	nam pla
lamington tray	2 cm-high baking tray
plain flour	all-purpose flour
prawns, green	shrimp, raw
sambal oelek	chilli paste
snake bean	long bean
snow peas	mange tout
soft brown sugar	light brown sugar
sweet potato	kumera

This edition published in 2003 by Bay Books, an imprint of Murdoch Magazines Pty Limited, GPO Box 1203, Sydney NSW 2001, Australia.

Managing Editor: Karen Hammial.
Food Editors: Kerrie Ray, Tracy Rutherford.
Editor: Wendy Stephen.
Designer: Michele Lichtenberger.
Recipe Development: Michelle Earl, Jo Richardson, Dimitra Stais.
Food Stylist: Georgina Dolling.
Photographers: Jo Filshie, Reg Morrison (Steps).
Food Preparation: Wendy Goggin, Jo Richardson.
Chief Executive: Juliet Rogers.
Publisher: Kay Scarlett.

ISBN 0 86411 468 0.
Reprinted 2004. Printed by Sing Cheong Printing Co. Ltd. PRINTED IN CHINA.

1 cm
2 cm
3 cm
4 cm
5 cm
6 cm
7 cm
8 cm
9 cm
10 cm
11 cm
12 cm
13 cm
14 cm
15 cm
16 cm
17 cm
18 cm
19 cm
20 cm
21 cm
22 cm
23 cm
24 cm
25 cm